When Every Day Is Saturday

The Retirement Guide for Boomers

Second, Revised Edition

Richard E. Grace

Purdue University Press
West Lafayette, Indiana

Previously published as *When Every Day is Saturday: Planning for a Happy Retirement*, 2002.
Purdue University Press edition, 2010.

Printed in the United States of America.

Library of Congress Cataloging-in-Publication Data

Grace, Richard E.
  When every day is Saturday : the retirement guide for boomers / by Richard E. Grace.
-- Rev. 2nd ed.
    p. cm.
  ISBN 978-1-55753-502-3 (alk. paper)
  1. Retirement. 2. Retirement--Planning. I. Title.
  HQ1062.G73 2009
  646.7'9--dc22
                               2009008435

This is, in part, a work of fiction. Although inspired by actual events and quotations, the names, persons, places, and characters are inventions of the author. Any resemblance to people living or deceased is purely coincidental.

Cover photograph © Catherine Yeulet / istockphoto.com (file # 7983929).

To Connie, my caring and supportive wife for over fifty years: We will continue to explore and discover life together for many more years to come!

To my former students: This is the lecture you helped me prepare, but you've never heard it. Now that you're ready, enjoy!

To my retired colleagues and friends: Thanks for participating and for sharing your wonderful stories about retirement. You're great!

I shall be telling this with a sigh
Somewhere ages and ages hence:
Two roads diverged in a wood, and I—
I took the one less traveled by,
And that has made all the difference.

Robert Frost
The Road Not Taken [1916], st. 4

Contents

List of Tables

Foreword

Dick Grace's retirement guide is a straight shooter: easy to use and right on target.

The Grace Retirement Inventory (GRI) will uncover your attitudes about freedom, finances, work, relocation, health and volunteerism. These factors will shape your future.

Retirement planning has never been so easy!

—Gene Cernan, Apollo Astronaut

Acknowledgments

I am especially indebted to the leadership of the Purdue University Retirees Association (PURA), who encouraged and supported this exploratory research on retirement. Further, I wish to thank the management of the Tippecanoe Laboratories of Eli Lilly and Company in Lafayette, Indiana. Participation of Lilly retirees added a significant dimension to the retirement environment we are beginning to understand.

Special thanks go to the Purdue University Press Editorial Board for their interest in this contemporary research and to the Press staff for their generous help with design, production, and marketing of this second edition.

In particular I wish to thank Kevin R. Kelly, my teacher and mentor, for his inspiration; Esther Gordon for her sound editorial advice; Cindi Rooze for her careful preparation of the original manuscript; Chad Pulver for help with data processing; Greg Smith and David Reuter for reading selected chapters; and my wife, Connie, and daughter, Virginia, for their patience, encouragement, and many suggestions. Sincere thanks also go to my many friends whose lively discussions helped to make this book a reality.

Chapter 1

Introduction: The Crystal Ball

Boomers, are you ready for the retirement environment? Chances are good that your response is "not quite," or perhaps "not yet," maybe even "not for me"! Those answers are quite normal, because there is always an uncertainty about change that gives us pause. For most of us, retirement looks like a major change in our career, a new beginning to the final third of our lives. And with this new beginning there are new questions—personal questions—which need to be worked through.

Why? We see that some retirees seem to have failed badly; many others appear to be happy and content. This latter group has found a good measure of fulfillment with their new lifestyle. What was their guide to success?

Years before my first retirement, I started asking my already-retired friends: "What have you learned about retirement"? and "What questions should I be asking myself now"? Their responses, usually, were brief, often obtuse. However, the following patchwork finally emerged with a general priority as follows:

1. Are you going to move to another community?
2. Can you retire cold turkey, or will you need some kind of transition with your work?
3. What are you going to retire *to*?
4. What happens if you live too long?

These four questions, without answers, were the starting point for my own retirement planning. Reading produced little new information, except for the four M's: Money, Money, Money, and Medicare. My conclusion was that retirement either was much too easy or it was far too complicated for me to understand. I didn't retire and went back to work for five additional years.

During that time I got hooked on retirement intellectually and set some immediate goals:

- To define retirement as quantitatively as I could;
- To explore transitions that may occur around the time of retirement;
- To learn enough so that my wife and I could ease into our own retirement; and
- To offer help and advice to others considering retirement.

This short book will help you work through the very personal process of discovering what's likely to be consequential to your happiness in retirement. If this pledge seems like gazing into a crystal ball, it is. You'll see the results of my exploration and discovery with seven hundred retirees who shared their attitudes about retirement. In fact, careful analysis of their views led to the discovery of eternal Saturdays, precisely those ideas and concepts which retirees value the most.

Finally, what this book is *not* about:

1. Aging. This book deals with men and women approaching retirement age, generally age fifty-five to seventy, with a focus on pre- and post-retirement concerns, not on gerontology.
2. Self-Help Rules. This book will help you explore and discover personal attitudes, which are integral to retirement planning and retirement living. There are no specific rules.
3. Professional Services. Your life may change based on the information about retirement in this book. However, health concerns, financial and legal matters, human sexuality, marriage, religion, and other related subjects may require separate interventions by licensed professional personnel.

In short, you are invited to discover new information about yourself that will make the next stage of your life full of purpose and happiness. In particular, you will answer six of the most important questions about the next phase of your working life—your retirement!

Chapter 2

Your Attitude, Your Future

Our attitudes normally are formed by a combination of past experiences, beliefs, values, needs, drives, motives—in short, by our cumulative experience and our personality. Since attitudes normally create intentions, and intentions prompt subsequent actions and activities, your attitude toward retirement really matters. It will shape your future!

Retirement is a life event—a change in lifestyle that prompts a need for readjustment. You probably have experienced many wonderful life events already: marriage, children, career changes, promotions, and success in business. You also may have experienced some unpleasant life events: divorce, death of a child, cancer, caregiving for elderly parents, and investments turned sour. The common element in all of these life events is a transition period of readjustment. So it is with retirement, which often requires a transition period of a few months to a year or more for readjustment.

In order to explore attitudes about retirement, I created a survey instrument, field-tested it with friends and colleagues, and perfected trial statements to insure very broad coverage of the retirement environment. Seven hundred retirees voluntarily completed this comprehensive survey instrument. The retirees represented a full spectrum of hourly-rate workers (approximately 260 clerical, service, trades, and support workers) as well as salaried employees (approximately 440 supervisors, faculty, managers, and professionals). Their age ranged from 51 to 95 years, and their annual household income varied from under $15,000 to over $200,000.

Retirees were invited to express their attitudes about 60 current life situations. Their responses varied from "strongly agree" to "strongly disagree" in five increments. I analyzed their responses with a statistical method called "Exploratory Factor Analysis" and discovered six specific themes or domains. These domains express the attitudes of the respondents succinctly: What really matters to retirees?

Now, it's your turn. What's really important to you about retirement?

Grace Retirement Inventory (GRI)

The Grace Retirement Inventory (GRI) is a concise evaluation of probable success in retirement. Self-scored and self-interpreted, the GRI has been designed for men and women approaching retirement age, normally around age 55 to 70. Individual results are developed for six major themes, or domains, in the retirement environment. In every case the reader's domain scores are compared to normative scores from 700 retirees. This provides a quantitative evaluation of the reader's attitude toward retirement, as well as the reader's probable success in retirement.

For most individuals, the results will apply to the first decade of retirement. However, circumstances change with each of us, and thus do our attitudes. The principal focus of the GRI is on the transition from the workforce to retirement. Equally important life events such as the death of a parent, death of a spouse, or remarriage may alter our attitudes about retirement significantly.

This survey contains 37 short statements about ordinary life situations. Please read each statement carefully and mark one of the numbers immediately below it. The code for Statements 1-37 is as follows:

A = Strongly disagree, most definitely false
B = Disagree
C = Neutral, not sure
D = Agree
E = Strongly agree, most definitely true

Please evaluate each item individually; mark in only one response—your personal response—to each statement. Add your scores for each group of items as directed.

Table 2.1 Grace Retirement Inventory (GRI)

Will you enjoy the Retirement Environment? When you respond to each item, please use this scale:

A	B	C	D	E
Strongly disagree	Disagree	Neutral, not sure	Agree	Strongly agree

Example: If you "agree" with Statement 1, you would circle "4."

1. I will really like the freedom that comes with being retired.

    1   2   3   4   5

2. I value keeping busy.

    1   2   3   4   5

3. I have sufficient drive and energy to start new projects.

    1   2   3   4   5

4. I enjoy good health.

    1   2   3   4   5

5. I like to learn something new every day.

    1   2   3   4   5

6. I am optimistic about the future.

    1   2   3   4   5

7. During the last year, I enjoyed a vacation away from home.

    1   2   3   4   5

8. My family and I will enjoy my retirement years.

    1   2   3   4   5

9. I will not be bored with retirement.

    1   2   3   4   5

10. Hobbies are an important part of my life.

    1   2   3   4   5

Add your scores for items 1-10 and record here: _____

11. My retirement income will be greater than my expenses.

1   2   3   4   5

12. My retirement income will provide for all my needs.

1   2   3   4   5

13. I will be able to travel wherever I choose to go.

1   2   3   4   5

14. I will have sufficient income to pay all my bills.

1   2   3   4   5

15. I could afford to live in a nursing home for an extended period.

1   2   3   4   5

16. Compared to pre-retirement, my income will be about the same.

1   2   3   4   5

Add your scores for items 11-16 and record here: _____

17. When I retire, I expect to feel anxiety and separation.

5   4   3   2   1

18. I plan to work beyond the normal retirement age.

5   4   3   2   1

19. I will adjust easily to retirement.

1   2   3   4   5

20. I will be bored with retirement.

5   4   3   2   1

21. I plan to work part-time as a transition to full retirement.

1   2   3   4   5

22. I should retire early.

1   2   3   4   5

23. My spouse/significant other thinks I should retire early.

1   2   3   4   5

Add your scores for items 17-23 and record here: _____

24. I do not want to move away from my family and friends.

    1   2   3   4   5

25. I am considering relocation to a different community.

    5   4   3   2   1

26. I plan to reside permanently in my current community.

    1   2   3   4   5

27. I would like to own a vacation home in a different climate.

    1   2   3   4   5

Add your scores for items 24-27 and record here: _____

28. I worry about having health problems.

    1   2   3   4   5

29. I am fearful of getting cancer.

    1   2   3   4   5

30. Depression has been a problem for me.

    5   4   3   2   1

31. My weight has increased in recent years.

    1   2   3   4   5

32. I balance diet and exercise to keep my weight under control.

    1   2   3   4   5

33. Regular exercise keeps me fit.

    1   2   3   4   5

Add your scores for items 28-33 and record here: _____

34. Volunteering a few hours every week is important to me.

    1   2   3   4   5

35. I volunteer regularly for community service activities.

1   2   3   4   5

36. I have taken on too many volunteer activities.

1   2   3   4   5

37. Religious activities are an important part of my life.

1   2   3   4   5

Add your scores for items 34-37 and record here: _____

Let Me Count the Ways

Now you can compare your results to those who created the database—over 700 retirees. Perhaps you will identify what areas need additional planning, and perhaps you will find assurance that you are quite ready to retire in the immediate future.

Here's how. Table 2.2 identifies the retirement domains and rank-orders them by importance to the 700 retirees surveyed. Are you surprised by this order?

Table 2.2 The Retirement Domains

Rank	Domain	Items
1.	Freedom and Leisure (F & L)	1 - 10
2.	Finances (F)	11 - 16
3.	Work (W)	17 - 23
4.	Family and Friends (F & F)	24 - 27
5.	Health (H)	28 - 33
6.	Helping Others (HO)	34 - 37

Next, go to Table 2.3 and familiarize yourself with the six horizontal bars. Each scale is different and represents one of the retirement domains.

Transfer your domain scores to each of the corresponding horizontal bars. For example, if your Freedom and Leisure score is 41, mark an "x" at 41 on the F & L scale.

The central range—the **Average Range**—represents the scores of approximately two-thirds of the retiree population. The other third of the scores falls either in the High Range or the Low Range; an occasional score may exceed the scale markings. High domain scores indicate great potential satisfaction with being retired. Low domain scores indicate an emotional struggle with some aspect of retirement; low domain scores also suggest the need for some additional planning, before or after retirement.

Table 2.3 The Retirement Scoreboard

Freedom and Leisure (F & L)

25 • • • • 30 • • • • 35 • • • • 40 • • • • 45 • • • • 50

Finances (F)

5 • • • • 10 • • • • 15 • • • • 20 • • • • 25 • • • • 30 •

Work (W)

10 • • • • 15 • • • • 20 • • • • 25 • • • • 30 • • • • 35

Family and Friends (F & F)

• 5 • • • • 10 • • • • 15 • • • • 20 • •

Health (H)

5 • • • • 10 • • • • 15 • • • • 20 • • • • 25 • • • • 30 •

Helping Others (HO)

• 5 • • • • 10 • • • • 15 • • • • 20 • •

Chances are that your scores are average-to-high in several domains and perhaps low in one or more domains. Location on the bars is your preliminary guide. The first principle to use in your interpretation of domain scores is as follows: **All domain scores correlate positively with happiness in retirement.** A more positive score indicates a higher degree of happiness in your future retirement.

There is a second principle to keep in mind as you think about your newly-found domains. This principle deals with the stability of your domain scores over time: **All domains are stable for the first decade of retirement. This time period is the happiest for most retirees**.

The third principle involves gender. The domains represent all retirees, male and female alike: **All domain scores are independent of gender. Domain scores are the same for men and women.**

How did you do? Are you likely to be satisfied or dissatisfied with your future retirement?

The Next Steps

Savor your results! No one knows your scores but you. These are your indicators of a purposeful, meaningful, and fulfilling retirement.

You may wish to discuss your scores with your spouse, close friends, or relatives. If you can describe your scores and their simple interpretation, you have completed a major hurdle in your planning. You also should find that new questions will arise. Answers to these—your answers—also will add to your eventual happiness in retirement.

You should sample any or all of the next six chapters to learn more about specific content of the retirement domains. I recommend this especially if you have any low domain scores. These are clues that your future happiness may depend upon your thinking through some specific concerns about your future retirement environment.

Conclusions about the retirement environment are found in chapter 11. The methodology is as old as Socrates himself: six simple questions will guide you toward a successful retirement. Each question has many personal facets—and answers—most of which are illustrated later in this book. Simply put, your future happiness in retirement will depend on the thoughtfulness of *your own personal answers*.

If you wish to understand some of the background that was used to create the database, continue with the appendices. Appendix A offers you the opportunity to share your GRI scores and some demographic information for my ongoing research program on retirement transitions. Appendix B gives a brief technical discussion of the survey results. Appendix C shows the methodology for determining both the reliability and the validity of the GRI. If you are an investigative person, these appendices will be both instructive and entertaining for you to review.

Chapter 3

Freedom—You've Earned It

- I will really like the freedom that comes with being retired.
- I value keeping busy.
- I have sufficient drive and energy to start new projects.
- I enjoy good health.
- I like to learn something new every day.
- I am optimistic about the future.
- During the last year, I enjoyed a vacation away from home.
- My family and I will enjoy my retirement years.
- I will not be bored with retirement.
- Hobbies are an important part of my life.
- I can't wait to see what the next few years will bring.
- Reading new books and magazines always interests me.
- I have enjoyed a movie in the last few months.
- I enjoy a glass of wine or beer.

Freedom. Dreams. Lifestyle. Choices. Time. Sound interesting? Add values, family, health, and optimism in whatever measures are right for you. However you choose to enjoy your freedom, it will be the most important, the most precious part of your retirement.

Let's be practical. At first, freedom will mean no early morning alarms, no schedules or evening shifts, no office politics, no bosses, and no games with management. That's Freedom 101, weeks 1-8 or thereabouts.

There are deeper meanings to freedom in retirement. The principal freedom is control of your time. The next important is freedom of choice—how you will use your time meaningfully. Many retirees describe their new-found freedom as being able "to do what I want and when I want." The only editorial variation seems to be, "if I want."

A successful retirement normally is rooted in your work, your family, and your community. Of these, work and family, in either order, have been rooted for decades. These roots provide clues for using your freedom effectively.

If work is planning and doing, so is retirement. For some retirees, the only obvious planning seems to be, "Where will we eat out tonight?" The doing focuses on food alone. Six months into retirement finds these retirees 15 pounds heavier—up one dress size or about two inches in the waistband of their khakis.

For others, their days are filled with endless trips to the grocery store, the bank, the dry cleaners, post office, barber shop, hardware store, and even some comparison shopping at the local mall. Others add in a daily kaffeeklatsch to gossip and discuss "politics." Any number of retirees will tell you that they are busier now than when they were working.

Retirement *is* work but with the total freedom to choose and to schedule what you want to do and when you want to do it. And with this freedom come some responsibilities to yourself, to your family, and to your community.

Three principles to explore: How will you keep yourself physically active? Mentally alert? Optimistic about the future?

You—Nobody Else

Will you golf, garden, or just goof off? Retirees that I have interviewed offer a wide range of suggestions.

You need exercise of some type, so what will it be? Daily walks, a home workout program, a health club for swimming, or organized aerobics? Aerobic exercise is a fast way to burn calories and reduce your body fat, but beware of high-impact jogging unless your hips and knees are strong. The advantage of a health club, YMCA/YWCA, or local gymnasium is that they have equipment which offers you variety and choice.

Will you enter "senior games" at your city or county park? This, too, involves variety and choice, and liberal amounts of opportunity for socialization with others your own age. Freedom of choice is virtually limitless in the health arena.

Do you dance? You're never too old for swing. Did you ever wonder what happens to geriatric keyboarders? They play at pool parties for retiring Boomers. You can sip Chardonnay and slip into the pool to strains of Don Ho singing "Tiny Bubbles." And you don't have to dance very well, just dance!

Have you tried a massage? A Swedish massage? If you have muscle tension, reduced circulation, restricted movement, or even some pain, the long strokes, deep kneading, tapping, and rubbing by a massage therapist will relax you beyond your imagination.

One controversial health benefit is alcohol. Drinking small-to-moderate amounts of alcohol, perhaps one or at most two drinks per day, seems to reduce cardiovascular disease (heart attack, stroke) as well as to lower the overall death rate compared to non-drinkers. Drinking moderately surely is a choice that is now known to have a positive effect on middle-aged and elderly Americans. Is drinking in moderation a wise choice for you?

Do you read either the comics or Chekhov plays—maybe both? If so, that is a great habit; do keep reading and learning! The more you learn, the more you will want to learn. Exercise your brain, stretch it. Curiosity will prevent deterioration of your thinking processes. In turn, you will stay young. All of this thinking seems to be a good choice!

Have you voted by proxy on the Internet? Another great choice for many stockholders. Or perhaps you need beginning instruction in basic computer skills. These and many other types of instruction are available at local community colleges and other institutions. Can you afford to ignore your intellectual choices?

> Every day I want to learn something new—living is constant learning and enjoyment.
> —Constance, age 82, retired at age 70

> Read, read, read.
> —Stan, age 78, retired at age 68

> Change fields, activities, projects, reduce work time as needed… but don't stop. Keep yourself active and make contributions in all

four areas of human need…physical, mental, social-emotional, and spiritual.

—Bjorn, age 75, retired at age 70

Your Family and Friends

Optimism about your future often involves family and friends. What have you considered recently that involves others? A community organization, a new hobby, or a vacation home where family and friends are welcome? Whom do you travel with—your spouse or significant other, perhaps another couple?

Travel is the principal choice of many retirees, especially in the early years of their retirement. Florida beaches call, big cities clamor, state and national parks whisper, Hawaii sings. Of course, the costs vary depending on where you stay, what you eat, and what you buy. More freedom of choice!

Caribbean waters normally are smooth as glass; perhaps you and your spouse or significant other would enjoy a short cruise to San Juan. For first-time "world travelers," London is an easy trip, with side excursions to Stratford-on-Avon and Stonehenge. For the adventuresome, Incan ruins in Machu Picchu, the Great Wall in Beijing, or safari in Kenya.

Whatever your budget—Yellowstone, New York City, or a camping trip 50 miles from home—a travel getaway will promote both physical health and mental growth.

Keeping up with old friends is something that most retirees count as a prime benefit of their after-work years. Finally, there is time to make that long telephone call, write a chatty letter, or send a quick e-mail.

Your Community

There is both a need and a niche for you in community affairs. Both the need and the niche cut both ways; you will enjoy serving, and those whom you help will benefit from your efforts.

What abilities and interests do you have that your community needs? Your community needs your time and your talent now. Can you offer a few hours of volunteer effort to a social service agency, a local hospital, or a community center for kids? Does your church office need repairs or secretarial services? Are there opportunities at thrift shops or soup kitchens? Can you pound a nail straight enough for Habitat for Humanity? If not, could you learn?

Above all, remember that you can change activities as you wish; you can try new ones and switch if they turn out to be less than you anticipated. It's a smorgasbord out there!

You may be a workaholic or perhaps you need the income. Let's just say you like the discipline of the workplace. In that case, get a part-time job after you retire. You'll enjoy some socialization and keep busy at the same time. And 10 or 20 hours a week will soon send a signal to you as to whether you have made the right choice in your new line of work.

> If you have no hobbies or other interests, keep working.
> —Chad, age 58, retired at age 52

> Retire as soon as possible. Indeed, there is life after work!
> —Jacob, age 60, retired at age 55

> I work part-time in the plumbing department of a local retail store, approximately 10 hours weekly. This part-time job is something I enjoy very much and have been doing for four years.
> —Patrick, age 54, retired at age 50

Freedom's Twin: Flexibility

Throughout your entire life you have experienced ups and downs, changes you made and changes that just happened to you. Each turn of the world brought new situations, and somehow or other, you managed. You are still here.

The secret has been your flexibility, your bending into the wind and dealing with change. Retirement calls on you to be as flexible as ever—to meet new challenges, to try new experiences, to meet your spouse more than halfway, to make new friends, and to seek adventure and fulfillment when the old ways just don't cut it anymore.

What makes flexibility in retirement more accessible is that the stakes are not as high as they used to be. You can change your mind when you want to and dump activities and situations that annoy you, even people who get on your nerves.

You can try something new in sports, hobbies, politics, religion, volunteerism, and more. Nothing is engraved in stone!

> It has been a most positive time in my life. My motto: I was born to retire!
>> —Lloyd, age 73, retired at age 65

> Have fun, enjoy your good health, live every day of your life with passion.
>> —Clark, age 60, retired at age 52

> Seize the moment;
> Travel, see friends, visit children far away,
> Eat out, have fun, follow your dreams.
> Commune with God,
> Help your fellow man.
>> —Myra, age 72, retired at age 59

My Personal Space: Freedom—You've Earned It!

Think small, think big, dream, explore fantasy, be introspective, then get real and make a written list of three new ventures that you really would like to experience in the next five years. Even better, share your thoughts with your spouse or significant other and prepare a joint written list. What would you like to do together? Consider the motivation, the obstacles, the rewards, and keep your list for reference. Perhaps you'll revise it, perhaps not. Enjoy your freedom, you've earned it!

FREEDOM AND CHOICE: WHAT SOME RETIREES SAY...

I am very busy and don't have a spare moment. Retirement is a wonderful experience! I enjoyed my work experience, but retirement is the best of all worlds. I set my own schedule; I can be creative and have the pleasure of completing many worthwhile projects. My wife and I have enjoyed good health, and we still love each other after 48 years of marriage.

My advice to younger people is to develop interesting hobbies outside regular work. One must retire *to* something.

Don't vegetate! Be active!

—Garth, age 72, retired at age 65

My retirement is enjoyable. I don't have to hurry much anymore. I'm able to visit friends and relatives more now. I can give more of my time to my church. I'm reading a lot more, visiting the public library. Think about how you will spend your time, then do it!

—Midge, age 68, retired at age 65

I love retirement! At first it felt as though I were on vacation. I have kept in touch with the people I worked with and enjoy their company still. I am as busy as I want to be at this time. I may stay up all hours if I wish to, which I never felt that I could do while working. Retirement is what you make of it—different people have different needs, and should plan and act accordingly.

—Tina, age 64, retired at age 63

I love every day of my retirement! It gives me the time to bowl, golf, shop, and work in my yard. And when winter comes, I sit, early in the morning, with my cup of coffee and my newspaper and watch it snow outside. Later, I often meet friends for lunch or dinner. It's a great life! I highly recommend it!

—Pamela, age 76, retired at age 52

Relief! I am enjoying reduction of pressure to meet deadlines; opportunities to travel out-of-season; sleeping late when I feel like it; more time for friends and family; more time for volunteer opportunities in the community (and there are lots of them!).

—Gwen, age 72, retired at age 66

The best part of retirement is being able to do all the things I previously had to do on the weekend during the week. I am also able to walk for an hour every morning. The worst part is the increase in out-of-pocket costs for medical insurance and for prescriptions.

—Caitlin, age 65, retired at age 64

My wife and I spend as much time as possible with our children and their families. We live in the same residence we had during our employment. We travel to warmer locations during the winter and cooler ones during the summer. I can read a lot and do gardening in the summer. Having worked until I was 70, I miss work and my colleagues very little. The transition to retirement has been a happy event.

—Kelley, age 73, retired at age 70

Travel, reading, photography, professional contacts, and meetings keep us young and satisfied.

—Larry, age 70, retired at age 67

Life is change. Make plans, knowing that they will probably change, too. Be flexible. By the time you learn to live, it's time to die!

—Pauline, age 56, retired at age 52

After my first wife died, I took a year's leave of absence to make sure retirement was what I wanted. It was, so I officially retired the next year. The biggest surprise was that I am as busy after retirement as before.

—Kevin, age 64, retired at age 59

Freedom is marvelous. Choice is challenging. Opportunity is open. Retirement counseling is available, if needed.

—Booth, age72, retired at age 65

The best part of retirement for me has been the freedom to travel, spend time with family, and select projects to work on which are enjoyable. The time to garden, read, and occasionally watch television programs or videos has been a big bonus.

The worst part has been some health problems, including aches and pains of the passing years. A tendency to over-program is slowly coming under control.

—Marian, age 71, retired at age 65

My husband and I did quite a bit of traveling for about 10 years, until I lost him. Since then I spend quite a bit of time at a Senior Center. I enjoy doing crafts and needlework and being out with people. I am thankful that I can still drive my car.

My advice would be to keep busy—either with hobbies or volunteering for something you enjoy doing. *Do something that gives you a reason to get up in the morning.*

—Corabelle, age 81, retired at age 63

Before I retired I made a list of things to do to keep me busy with all the free time I anticipated; I have never gotten to the list. I like retirement a lot!

—Riley, age 69, retired at age 57

Have a list of new activities—try them out and add to the list. Spend time to help the kids and grandkids. Have finances figured out well before retirement. Continue learning and develop new skills. Slow down, smell the roses, there is no one to impress, unless they're still working. Be thankful! Retirement is a recent development and only happens in industrialized countries like the USA. Freedom provides the best of opportunities.

—Jake, age 57, retired at age 52

The best is being retired. Don't need to get out on cold or bad days. The worst is to stay at home too much. Have to watch your income to be sure it will pay all the bills.

You have a lot of TV, fishing, yard, and garden time. I love it.

—Chester, age 80, retired at age 65

Enjoy not having to go to work, especially not having to work nights, which I did for 12 years. I still do not sleep right at night.

—Abner, age 63, retired at age 58

We have kept very busy with lodge work, yard work, and house. We also help others. Travel somewhat and winter in Florida. I have really enjoyed not working.

—Rita, age 60, retired at age 53

If the weather is bad, just stay indoors. I used to hate the winter, but not anymore. I don't have to shovel snow as often as I have to mow the lawn.

—Edison, age 67, retired at age 55

My wife is a voracious reader and is a great patron of library book sales. She derives a great deal of pleasure each year from watching a wide variety of wild flowers pop up in her rather large wild flower bed. Our backyard is carpeted with Spring Beauties, and it can't be mowed in the spring until they have gone to seed. Do you know very many retirees who don't grow tomatoes? I grow mine in half whiskey barrels in soil that has known nothing but tomatoes for years. Not an approved technique by agronomists, but the fruit is sweet and plentiful.

—Joel, age 78, retired at age 58

After retiring we sold our house and everything in it. We purchased a motor home and have been on the road since. We return to Indiana for the Indy 500 and then for the Brickyard 400. We have visited 18 states and are currently in Arizona. We plan to continue this as long as possible.

—Parrish, age 55, retired at age 55

We have lived in south Florida from six-to-ten months a year since retirement. My wife and I square dance two-to-three times a week during the winter months. I took up woodcarving about two years after retirement. Now I teach woodcarving about ten hours a week during the winter months.

—Chuck, age 68, retired at age 57

Chapter 4

Plan, Plan, Plan

- My retirement income will be greater than my expenses.
- My retirement income will provide for all my needs.
- I will be able to travel wherever I choose to go.
- I will have sufficient income to pay all my bills.
- I could afford to live in a nursing home for an extended period.
- Compared to pre-retirement, my income will be about the same.
- Compared to pre-retirement, my expenses will be about the same.
- My health insurance is excellent.

Are you a saver? Enrolled in a company pension plan? Your own 401(k), IRA, or Keogh? Are you a willing investor in stocks and mutual funds? Eligible for Social Security? Expect a family inheritance?

What's your plan? Whether you are a single parent at the poverty threshold, a married couple in the "big middle," or a corporate executive at the top, you need a plan for your financial future.

Your home equity gain may be impressive; it's an important asset, one that should be free and clear at retirement, but it won't spin off much cash. And all the anecdotal advice from friends and co-workers about picking the right mutual fund probably won't create great wealth either. What you need is a comprehensive plan—your plan—and once you have created it, you need to check the plan, work the plan, and revise the plan until you take your last breath.

Why a plan? Two reasons:

• A plan will enable you to accumulate wealth from a variety of sources, especially during your working years.
• A plan also will enable you to draw the income you will need during your retirement years.

Neither reason can be ignored in your pre-retirement or in your post-retirement planning. Your financial future depends on the soundness of your plan as well as your ability to manage it, sometimes with a bit of serendipity.

You saw in chapter 3 that personal freedom was the most important aspect of retirement. An overwhelming 93% of retirees agreed that personal control of their time and activities is what makes retirement so special; only 6% of retirees were dissatisfied with some aspect of their new-found freedom.

The second most important aspect of retirement is financial independence. Some retirees equate financial freedom with the ability to do what they want—including giving to others. Other retirees describe financial freedom as the essence of life, freedom from worry or stress, even as the payoff from their working years. While two-thirds of retirees agree that they have financial freedom, 26%—one-in-four retirees—do not believe that they have the financial freedom they anticipated. So, a few words to the wise:

> Be sure you have adequately planned for financial independence. The rest comes easy.
>
> —Matthew, age 72, retired at age 67

> The most important thing to do to insure a comfortable and enjoyable retirement is to plan for it financially. This provides the independence to do what you enjoy.
>
> —Chris, age 61, retired at age 59

> My advice to those considering retirement is to be certain that you are financially secure. It would be a shame to have all the time needed to travel or to do whatever you wish and not the funds to do so.
>
> —Judy, age 65, retired at age 64

My wife and I started planning our retirement when we were in our late 30s. We made investments and purchased a home on the Gulf of Mexico for winter living during retirement. Retirement has offered us a chance to travel and do all the things we put off during our working years.

—Corey, age 63, retired at age 58

My disappointment with retirement is that my wife feels I should have worked another year or two to have more assurance of our financial future. My advice is to anticipate more spending in retirement. We have more time so we buy more, vacation more, eat out more, etc. We are definitely spending more money in retirement than we expected.

—Chad, age 59, retired at age 57

Start planning very early. Systematic saving is the key for the needed income of retirement.

—Chester, age 60, retired at age 53

I've found my health has improved since retirement. I'm starting to notice that my retirement income is losing ground to the cost of living.

—Merritt, age 61, retired at age 55

Since my retirement—the first year I did things around the house, gardening, yard work, repair of house projects. The second year I got a part-time job, three days a week. The third year, I started working full-time, 40-plus hours a week, and have been doing that ever since. I could not maintain the same standard of living without added income.

—Roger, age 59, retired at age 54

We have been on two cruises and several vacations during retirement, yet we never outgrow the need for more income.

—Hal, age 71, retired at age 57

I retired much earlier than I had long anticipated because of a radical shift in administrative procedures within my area. By doing, of course, I foreclosed on a significant amount of income and insurance benefits. I now wish that I had sucked it up and stuck it out...

—Jesse, age 73, retired at age 60

I feel much better; my wife has even noticed the improvement. Advice for people planning retirement: start planning five-to-ten years in advance. Get finances in order and you won't experience any problems. As long as finances are in good order, get out as early as possible. There is so much more to life than working.

—Dolph, age 54, retired at age 53

It's Time to Get Serious

With luck, the children have finished school; they also have jobs and are out on their own. You have helped pay tuition, room, and board for years. Student loan repayments are your kids' problems. Your youngest daughter expects you to finance most of her wedding plans in about two years. With a bit more luck you will miss the "yo-yo" syndrome—a recently divorced child moving home to "get back on their feet."

Your parenting expenses are more or less over. It's time to get serious about your own financial future. You have 10 years, plus or minus, to sock it away for retirement. It's time to be a bit selfish!

Your Current Income

What's your annual income? If you are an "average" married couple family, your annual income falls in one of these ranges:

Age	Annual Income
35 - 44 years	$70,000 - 80,000
45 - 54 years	$76,000 - 86,000
55 - 64 years	$66,000 - 76,000
65 - 74 years	$45,000 - 55,000

If you are a single male householder, you probably fall into the $40,000 - $45,000 range, and if you are a single female householder, you are well above average if you exceed $35,000 annually.

How much have you been able to save every month? $100? $200? $500 or more? Where do you invest your savings? That's one of the key questions you need to answer correctly in order to achieve some measure of financial independence.

Your Net Worth

What do you own and what is it worth—realistically? Chances are good that you have a checking account, a savings account, equity in your home and a motor vehicle or two, and shares of stock in a mutual fund. You also may own some U.S. savings bonds or equity in real estate or a business. Forget about your clothing, kitchen utensils, jewelry, and furniture, unless it is heirloom-quality.

What's it all worth? First, identify your principal assets and estimate their present value. Then deduct your liabilities, such as bank loans on your house and vehicles, credit card debt, and other outstanding bills. The sum of your assets minus your liabilities usually is called your net worth. It's not a very precise measure, but it is an estimate of what you own, free and clear.

If you are a married couple, age 55-to-64, you probably own around $170,000 to $190,000 with your home equity at 55 to 65% of the total. Of course, the range of American households is enormous; young American households (under 35 years) often have a net worth of zero while older households (over 65 years) often report $500,000 and more.

In addition to your net worth you may have some future interests, such as a pension plan or a life insurance policy. You also may be eligible for Social Security when you retire. Because these are future interests, they are not normally included in your net worth estimate.

Net worth doesn't put food on the table or pay the bills. Income does. Some of your assets just don't spin off any cash income. For example, your home equity just sits there on paper; if anything, your home costs you cash for upkeep, mortgage payments and taxes. Not a cash cow for sure!

What's Next?

Can you estimate what income you would need if you retired next year? Or in a decade? What will change? Will the mortgage be paid off? Will you spend less on transportation or clothing? Perhaps more on health care? Travel? Eating out? If you cannot spot a change in your projected cost of living, perhaps you will need approximately the same annual income to start retirement as you have now.

One of life's defining moments is the day you get your final paycheck. Or the day you sell your business and close with the bank. *Finis—* or so it seems. How will you generate sufficient income to live the way you have? One answer is that you cannot—in which case you had better keep on working, like it or not. If, however, you have had a financial plan, and if you have worked your plan and checked your plan over the last 10-to-20 years, then you have saved, invested, and projected your annual income at retirement and beyond. Easy to say, harder to do, and does your projected retirement income match your dreams?

There are two financial principles to follow as you begin your planning in detail: **(1) Save regularly over and above your pension and your Social Security** and **(2) When you retire, you may choose to draw down your savings by 4% to 5% per year.** Odds are good that you will not outlive your nest egg.

Strategies for Saving

Let's start with the most important strategy of all: your attitude. Are you a regular saver? Do you transfer $25, $250, or $2,500 out of every paycheck to some type of savings or investment? Do you save only to clean out your account every few months, or do you save for the long haul—your retirement? In short, do you have a positive attitude toward saving?

What's your attitude toward risk? Toward a money market savings account versus a 401(k) account with shares of common stock or mutual funds? The difference is risk and how you live with it. Can you tolerate moderate ups and downs? Large variations in value? And how does your spouse's tolerance compare with your own?

Television ads, newspapers, magazines, direct mailings, and the Internet flood us with information about investing to secure financial independence—too many people willing to help you invest *your* money for *their* fees. My advice: *Caveat emptor* comes to mind.

Most of us, however, do need some guidance and specialized information about saving and investing, but first we need a personal plan to follow. Here are the suggested steps to follow:

1. Commit to a regular savings plan.
2. Save something every pay period.
3. Invest with different strategies (CDs, stocks, mutual funds, savings bonds, etc.).
4. Take risks commensurate with what you can handle emotionally.
5. Get help if you need it.
6. Project the income you need at retirement.

Strategy 1. Low Risk, Low Return. Checking and savings accounts, money market funds, and certificates of deposit offer the greatest security at the lowest risk. Can you afford to keep your money working at 1% to 5% for decades?

Strategy 2. Intermediate Risk, Intermediate Return. Can you handle some risk? Selected mutual funds, both stock and bond funds, U.S. bonds, and corporate and municipal bonds offer relatively little risk and pay 3% to 8% over the long haul. I know an elderly farm couple, now retired, who has invested $5 million in 6% bonds. Too cautious, yes! But these investors saw their parents and grandparents lose everything in 1929-1930.

Strategy 3. High Risk, High Return. Aggressively-managed mutual funds, global stock funds, growth and value funds, index funds, and individual stock accounts are readily available to the investor who can handle a variety of risks—read financial ups and downs. While any one of these equity investments may return 20% to 30% for a year or two (or longer), over the last seventy years equity growth has averaged 11.7%. The best of all strategies? Yes, when the bulls are running in the stock market. Yes, when you can handle a real loss of 20% to 30% (or more) of your savings as easily as you can handle the anticipated gain.

Retirement Plans

Fifty to sixty percent of full-time American workers have retirement plans sponsored by their employers. The larger the company, the higher the educational level and salary, the more likely the company will offer retirement benefits. Older Boomers often will have pension plans known as "defined benefit plans." These normally guarantee an exact dollar income based on a formula that includes your years of service, your peak salary for several years (often five years) just before retirement, and a small percentage factor (which varies with the company). As you can see, longevity on the job and a high salary close to retirement drive your retirement income up.

What do pension plans pay? On average, $10,000 to $15,000 annually, some more, some less. An average married couple at age 65 could expect an additional $18,000 annually from Social Security. A low-end wage earner family with virtually no pension and minimum Social Security might struggle with an annual retirement income of $12,000. A high-end average couple with a pension and Social Security might feel secure with their annual retirement income of $48,000. But many retirees will do much better than this. Who are they?

The regular savers—those with discipline, patience, and some tolerance for risk—will do much better than those who rely on a company pension and Social Security alone. There are several major opportunities for increasing your retirement income. Younger Boomers should increase their personal savings to a minimum of $4,000 to $5,000 annually, preferably more—considerably more, if they can. Where to invest those savings?

- If your employer offers a 401(k) plan, often called a "defined contribution plan," you should get your savings deducted automatically from your paycheck. Your savings are federal tax-deferred; you pay no income tax now, but you will on your future income at retirement. Many employers offer an additional percentage match to the money you invest in your 401(k) account. Best of all, your employer probably has selected a number of investment options for you to choose. That's where your tolerance for risk can really pay off (well, with some luck it will).

- If you work for a tax-exempt employer or a not-for-profit organization, you can save through a 403(b) program, which is virtually the same at the 401(k) program described above.
- If you are self-employed (for example, an author, consultant, or entrepreneur), you should consider a SEP IRA (Simplified Employee Pension Plan), a SIMPLE IRA (Savings Incentive Match Plan for Employees), or possibly one of the Keogh plans. SEPs and SIMPLEs are the easier to establish.
- Other variations of the Individual Retirement Account (IRA) might appeal to you as well: Traditional or Roth. As with all IRAs, there are eligibility and filing status requirements mandated by the IRS. My choice for younger savers or for those who expect to live very long lives is the Roth IRA. While your investments are made with after-tax dollars, at retirement you will draw tax-free income. If you choose a minimum distribution option when you retire, you can spread your draw and grow your investment for decades.

Get Help?

How is your attitude toward all this saving and investing? Crap shoot or comfort zone, your best option is to start with free advice from the benefits section of your company human relations office. If not there, go to your bank or savings and loan office. They'll give you plenty of free information and probably offer an opinion or two as well. If you have a friendly broker, a CPA, or an attorney, they will be an important re-source. If you're well-off, you might use a full-service brokerage house or a certified financial planner. They will help you for a fee that you should discuss in advance.

Income after Retirement

Have you been watching your savings grow? Your personal stock account? Your 401(k)? Are you salivating about the prospects for your re-tirement income? Or perhaps somewhat dejected?

There are financial facts of life you need to consider now; you can't afford to wait until retirement. Not only do you need to evaluate what your assets are (and might become), you need to project what annual income you might expect from them.

Bill and Betty

Bill (age 56) and Betty (age 54) have been married for 33 years. Bill attended a community college for two years and has been employed by a large electric utility company for nearly 30 years. He works as an electric operating supervisor.

Betty has worked for the last 12 years as a part-time salesperson in a major department store of a local shopping mall. Her hours are flexible, but seasonal demands normally are high and cause some conflict at home.

Bill and Betty own their own home and have accumulated approximately $85,000 of home equity over 25 years of mortgage payments and growth in value.

They both enjoy good health, although both will admit to eating too much and exercising too little.

Bill and Betty have two children, Bill Jr. and Christine. Bill Jr. graduated in Electrical Engineering Technology and Chris graduated in Nursing from their state university. They are both married, balance full-time work with child care, and are still repaying their student loans. They have two children each.

Bill and Betty provide no financial support to their children except for modest birthday and Christmas presents, primarily to the grandchildren.

Bill and Betty's Annual Income

(Ages 56 and 54, respectively)

Bill's earnings	$52,472
Betty's earnings	14,215
Dividends from mutual funds	2,120
Interest from savings	2,348
National Average	**$71,155**

Ted and Jean

Ted (age 68) was married at age 19 and divorced at age 21, no children.

This was a starter marriage that failed. Ted and Jean (age 65) have been married for 44 years. They are both high school graduates.

Ted has had a dual working life, first as an automobile mechanic, and for the last 28 years as an assembler in a transportation equipment plant making buses. He retired at age 66.

Jean has been employed on and off for the last 30 years as a part-time beautician in several different shops. She still works two days per week, mostly with standing appointments that she has had for years. Jean is ready to retire and give up her part-time earnings.

Ted and Jean have lived in a small subdivision for almost all of their married life. They purchased their house for $18,000, paid off their 30-year mortgage, and have current home equity of $110,000.

Ted and Jean have minor health problems. Ted has suffered hearing loss, probably from his occupational environments. He wears two hearing aids and is very uncomfortable in noisy bars because of peripheral sounds. Ted also has borderline high blood pressure and makes three trips to the bathroom every night due to an enlarged prostate. Jean is on medication for high cholesterol and has moderate arthritis in her hips and knees.

They have two married daughters who live out-of-state with their husbands and children. There are five children between the two families.

Ted inherited $45,000 in mutual funds and his parents' duplex and currently enjoys extra income from the two rental apartments. The mutual funds are valued at nearly $200,000 today. Ted and Jean are both concerned about the future for their five grandchildren. Neither daughter's family seems to be getting ahead financially, and they rely on Ted and Jean for occasional gifts, especially at holidays throughout the year. Ted and Jean are looking for ways to create more income for their own retirement years as well as to set something aside specifically for the grandchildren.

Ted and Jean's Annual Income

(Ages 68 and 65, respectively)

Pension	$10,831
Rent from duplex	12,000

Social Security	12,876
Jean's earnings	7,186
Dividends from stock accounts	3,784
Interest from savings	<u>2,800</u>
National Average	**$49,477**

Bill and Betty and Ted and Jean are hypothetical couples whose lives are typical and whose income matches the national averages. In order to understand their incomes in greater depth, you need to evaluate some potential cash returns on investments. These are summarized in Table 4-1.

Table 4-1 Investment Returns

Investment You Own	Your Annual Cash Return if Invested at Select Percentages		
Principal	2%	5%	10%
$50,000	$1,000	$2,500	$5,000
200,000	4,000	10,000	20,000
250,000	5,000	12,500	25,000
500,000	10,000	25,000	50,000
750,000	15,000	37,500	75,000
1,000,000	20,000	50,000	100,000

Bill and Betty Revisited a Decade Later

The biggest unknowns are, of course, future interests: Bill's pension, Betty's pension, Social Security, dividends, and interest income. Bill is in a 401(k) pension plan with a 50% company match; for every retirement dollar Bill puts in, the electric utility puts in $0.50 for the first 6% of his annual earnings. Bill's 401(k) is valued at approximately $275,000. Bill and Betty are hoping that it will double to $550,000 by the time Bill turns 67 and wants to retire.

Bill and Betty may need some funds at retirement for home repair or for travel. They could withdraw cash from Bill's 401(k) without penalty, subject only to IRS and the plan's withdrawal rules. The minimum distribution requirement (MRD) will kick in when Bill turns 70 ½. The benefits counselor at Bill's company can explain both the MRD and the rules in detail.

Let's assume that Bill draws down his 401(k) to $500,000 by the time he turns 70 ½. At that time, Bill and Betty will need to draw an MRD of approximately $18,200—and it will increase slightly every year.

Betty's Pension. Betty's working life has been in part-time jobs, and she has never qualified to join any company pension plan. Income: zero.

Social Security. In *current* dollars Bill will receive approximately $24,000 annually at age 67; Betty could elect to take approximately half of Bill's draw, $12,000 annually. Together, they might expect $36,000 annually. In fact, they may receive over $50,000 in *inflated* dollars at retirement. A scheduled session with the local Social Security office will provide all the necessary information.

Dividends. Conservative investors may get 2% cash dividends on common stock. Growth stocks average closer to 1% or even less. Bill and Betty currently enjoy $2,120 in annual dividends. If they average 2%, they have a broker account of $106,000, quite possibly more. If their equities double over the next decade, they can hope to double their dividend income by the time they retire.

Interest. CDs and money market accounts paid $2,348 last year. At 4%, their interest indicates nearly $59,000 socked away for a cash emergency. Seems high, but Bill and Betty are cautious savers. They won't add much cash in the next decade.

Bill (age 70 ½) and Betty's (age 68) Projected Annual Retirement Income

401(k) MRD	$18,200
Social Security (inflated)	54,000
Dividends	4,240
Interest	3,000
	$79,440

If they need more income, they could draw down their savings by 4% to 5% annually. Again, Bill's company benefits counselor or a bank advisor can offer free advice with different strategies. As often happens, the devil is in the details!

The most important part of this projection is how much better Bill and Betty will fare than Ted and Jean. The happy combination of higher income, careful savings, and the time value of their 401(k) really works!

Ted and Jean Revisited

Because Ted is retired and Jean is ready to retire, their income is relatively easy to analyze.

Pension. Ted worked for 28 years in an assembly plant, and his employer contributed regularly to a defined benefit pension plan. Based on their joint life expectancy, Ted and Jean's pension is $10,831 annually. This is "guaranteed" for life—but whose life, Ted or Ted *and* Jean? The mystery is, of course, the exact formula that determines the amount of the pension. The benefits counselor at Ted's plant holds all the critical information—including beneficiaries. Did Ted ever ask about the details? Will you?

Rent. Ted and Jean collect approximately $500 per month from each apartment in the duplex. Their gross annual rental income is $12,000.

Social Security. Ted's Social Security yields $12,876 annually. If Jean retires, she'll lose $7,186 in earnings, but will qualify for approximately $6,000 in Social Security. Jean needs a firm projection from the local Social Security office.

Dividends. Ted and Jean inherited some mutual funds and have been careful savers and investors. Their dividend income of $3,784 is based on mutual funds valued at nearly $200,000. If they had been more aggressive with growth stocks, their portfolio might be much larger, but their income would be about the same.

Interest. Ted and Jean enjoy cash savings of nearly $60,000. They regularly invest these funds in bank CDs between 3% and 5%. This results in interest income of $2,800 annually. They are thrifty and pay cash for everything!

And You?

Can you project your income at retirement age? You owe it to yourself to collect the necessary information and try. This is one more step toward "working your plan."

Chances are good you will need help with the details. That is where your company benefits counselor can provide free help. You can do your Social Security projection online or at the Social Security office—just make sure you understand the results. Your bank and broker will help you up to a point; then you may have to enlist some additional advice from a CPA or an attorney. You will also be smart to compare notes with some of your closest friends at work; they are asking the same questions you are!

New Expenses

Nearly every retiree takes a trip within the first year of their retirement. Rites of passage repeated! What will it be for you: fishing lodge or Caribbean cruise? Canoe or Crystal Symphony? The whole world is your universe, but the limiting feature may be what you can afford to spend or choose to spend.

While your retirement income may look good now, there are some financial changes headed your way. Your only savings may be in transportation costs to and from work and clothing costs for whatever "uniform" you have been wearing—blue jeans or blue pin-stripes.

Almost everything else you do will cost more than you have been spending. The first big ticket item is health care. You are no longer on the company plan; most likely, you are on Medicare Parts A, B, and D. And you will need a supplemental carrier to pick up items that Medicare doesn't cover. For a couple this will cost $2,000 to $5,000 annually, depending on the coverage they elect. Hot tip: Explore Medicare C—it may save you some money!

Housing should be a pretty flat cost until you decide you need a lake cabin or an RV or a Florida condominium. Surprise! You'll be newly-weds again (well, almost) and may need financing if you go beyond your means. Have fun, but it might be much cheaper to rent a few weeks and travel to new locations whenever wanderlust takes hold.

Entertainment costs are very personal: You know what you like to do best. With increased time, you will find that it is easy to spend more during retirement than you did in your latter working years. That is great if you treat the grandchildren or visit some dear friends. The only negative is your cash flow. Can your plastic or your savings handle the load?

If you undertake some serious remodeling projects, you will incur costs for materials and quite possibly for labor. OK on your cash flow? If you need help with your income tax preparation, that also will be an added cost annually. If you and your spouse need will and power of attorney (POA) documents prepared or updated, that, too, will impact your cash flow.

Wait until the estate planners come knocking. Some of them will have big ideas about your money. Certified financial planners can be very helpful, especially if you are having trouble saving. They'll also help you think through gifts to minors, second-to-die insurance policies, long-term nursing care policies, and even pre-paid funeral arrangements.

My suggestion: **Hang on to your money as long as you can. You might choose to spend it on yourself; you might *need* to spend it on yourself.**

I do recommend that you and your spouse update your wills and carefully give durable general power of attorney to each other, a relative, or other trusted friend. Further, you should execute a health care declaration and health care power of attorney under the living will laws of your state. Peace of mind after retirement is essential. And if you value your assets and your health as much as I do, your attorney will become your best friend.

Finally, inflation. You know that inflation has been under control for years (approximately 3%). You also should remember brief periods in your life when inflation raged at 15% and more. At 3% inflation, the price of a loaf of bread will take 24 years to double. At 6%, the price will double in 12 years. At 12%, 6 years. You may live another 25 years easily, maybe many more. Who will pay your bills when you get to be 75, 85, or 95 years old?

My Personal Space: Plan, Plan, Plan

Review your current annual income: salary, interest, dividends, other sources (rents, alimony, child support, veteran's benefits, disability ben-

efits, etc.). Construct a simple table and determine your current gross income. Does this match your Federal tax information?

Project your annual income after retirement. This may be a simple or complex tabular projection, and you may need to get some help. Your best choices are a benefits counselor in the human resources department where you work, your local bank or savings institution, and your local Social Security office.

Can you and your family survive on your projected annual retirement income? What can you do in the immediate future to increase your retirement income? Alternately, will you need to work part-time after retirement to supplement your income?

FINANCES: WHAT SOME RETIREES SAY...

> No surprises, I feel better than I have in years. Free advice, start planning for retirement from day one. I worked towards my retirement for 31 years, planned my money, and had no debts when I retired.
>
> —Romney, age 51, retired at age 49

> Plan finances above and beyond pension and Social Security.
>
> —Roseanne, age 95, retired at age 68

> Start planning your retirement income 15 to 20 years before you retire and stick with it.
>
> —Hank, age 75, retired age 67

> I have enjoyed my retirement very much. I was able to travel while I was still active and I was free from family obligations. I knew when I retired that I would need more income, so I concentrated on increasing my income. Fortunately, it was at a time when that could be done. I have quadrupled my income due to having a separate retirement account that made savings possible.
>
> —Beth, age 88, retired at age 64

My hardest adjustment since retiring has been going from working hard and saving all my life to spending money. I know that I have a large amount of money in investments and a 401(k) program, and I hesitate now to take money out even though that's what it was saved for.

—Jorge, age 59, retired at age 58

As a single person with no close family, I began to save for retirement 25 years before the event and continued to do so throughout the years of employment in addition to my pension plan and Social Security. I never made a major investment such as a home. I lived in apartments until 10 years after retiring when I moved into an independent living retirement community.

Suggestions:

1) Make long range pre- and post-retirement plans. Although they may need to be modified, they provide a solid base.

2) Make timely decisions, whether single or married, if any move is contemplated. Recognize that, on one hand, the years of active life of many people seem to be increasing; on the other hand, realities such as macular degeneration, Alzheimer's, and other degenerative diseases occur.

3) If interested in travel, do so in early retirement, because health or other conditions may make it difficult later.

—Gretchen, age 86, retired at age 66

Early retirement sounded good to us as it did to others, but if a person is young they should give it some serious thought. We have used more of our savings than I had expected; it is somewhat better now that I am on Social Security.

—Joe, age 62, retired at age 58

Be sure to include your spouse in your financial planning.

—Meyer, age 72, retired at age 62

Plan to have more money…

—Dora, age 80, retired at age 65

The biggest surprise was how we could make less money and do more things. I thought we might have to "do without," but nothing could be farther from the truth.

—Nicole, age 63, retired at age 61

I was fortunate in being able to retire at 57. Obviously I would not have this opportunity had it not been for my spouse's income and retirement package.

Initially, my time was spent taking care of sick parents. Now my husband and I are free to do pretty much what we want.

I'm still very busy as a paid church organist. I feel being active keeps me young in body and spirit. I'm very grateful for this opportunity to keep my mind working!

—Patricia, age 65, retired at age 57

Combining our love of travel with my experience in publishing has produced a "hobby" business that has grown into activity on a daily basis. Since retirement I have actively marketed our books and even had some success, reflected by active sales figures!

—Paul, age 69, retired at age 65

We have always lived within our income. My advice to future retirees is save up for retirement by contributing to 401(k) or other savings programs and being debt-free when you retire.

—Riley, age 67, retired at age 67

We decided not to annuitize our pension assets, at least for the time being. As a result of this departure from the "norm," we needed more information than was readily available. We enlisted the aid of an estate attorney, an accountant, and a broker, but the best assistance we received was from very candid conversations with recent retirees. We invited these couples into our home for dessert and coffee to learn what their experiences were upon retirement and where they were receiving their information from. We had to search out individuals who had solved some of the same problems we were facing. I believe there is a need for a mentoring group or a support group where small groups of individuals and their spouses could meet with others facing the same problems.

—Bill, age 68, retired at age 65

My husband and I have a motor home, and we have enjoyed traveling with no time constraints. We carefully saved as much as possible while we worked; now we are able to live comfortably and do anything we want.

—Margaret, age 66, retired at age 61

I ain't famous and I'm rich enough.

—Louise, age 80, retired at age 62

I'm not broke, but I'm not rich either. If not for the guidance of my boss, I would have been in a very bad way.

—Maribel, age 64, retired at age 62

For me retirement represented achieving the goal of being sufficiently financially independent so that I could focus on my objectives. I was no longer a slave to wages. I was "free at last" to do my own thing!

I have no shortage of meaningful things to try to get done before the grim reaper overtakes! I appreciate that the world will spin on and that there will be glorious sunrises and sunsets regardless of what I do or don't do.

A practical effect of automation is that there are fewer and fewer real wage paying jobs. This places an obligation on everyone, once they've met their basic needs, to get out of the way and leave those jobs to the young who really need them.

—Victor, age 67, retired at age 60

Thank heaven for Social Security—without it I'd be sacking groceries!

—Jim, age 85, retired at age 65

My major concern now is long-term nursing home expenses for both of us.

—Alvin, age 71, retired at age 61

Our income over 12 years has been level. Our main concerns are inflation and the increasing costs of medical and nursing home care. We are partially protected by long-time care insurance policies.

—Eric, age 82, retired at age 70

The worst was losing my spouse after 34 years of marriage. After I became accustomed to living without my husband, the best was the freedom to do as I chose. My biggest surprise was being able to live in our home and pay the bills with a little left over.

—Caroline, age 71, retired at age 55

Chapter 5

Early, Now, or Never

- When I retire, I expect to feel anxiety and separation.
- I plan to work beyond the normal retirement age.
- I will adjust easily to retirement.
- I will be bored with retirement.
- I plan to work part-time as a transition to full retirement.
- I should retire early.
- My spouse/significant other thinks I should retire early.
- I will miss daily contact with members of my department.

Retire early? Not so fast! There is much more to retirement than income, important though it is. In chapter 3 you found that the gift of freedom overshadows all other aspects of retirement; in chapter 4 you saw the importance retirees placed on income, the dreams of accumulating, and the realities of the pay-out.

The good news: 60% of all retirees report success in making a happy transition from work to retirement. The bad news: a disturbing 30% indicate lingering negative attitudes about retirement from their years in the workforce. Loss of socialization, loss of power, loss of income, and increased boredom and ennui may lower your self-esteem significantly after retirement.

Several key questions about your current work need consideration: Should I retire? When? With a transition or not? What's normal—or at least typical about retirement in my line of work?

You saw your parents and their contemporaries wait until age 65, followed by the obligatory retirement dinner, perhaps with the company watch or other memento. Right for them? Maybe. Right for you? Maybe, but there is much more freedom of choice that you should explore.

Retirement age is slowly decreasing for many reasons: health, income, working conditions, buy-outs, and force-outs. There is a principle you should follow to keep your retirement plans fluid: **Your retirement goal in the work domain is to retain control of your working life as long as possible.** With luck, *you* can make the final decision about when and how to leave your work. Alternately, you may lose control by a shift in company policy that will dictate your future to you.

The Early Ones

A good friend of many years retired at age 60 and told me, "It took me 20 minutes to adjust to retirement." Had she planned so carefully? Doubtful. Naive? Probably. Another good friend retired at age 63 and told me, "You get up one morning and ask, "Why am I going to work?" His planning and naivete are similar to my "20 minute" friend.

Some thoughtful consideration of alternatives will prompt your decision to stay on or to leave early. These concerns involve both positive and negative aspects of your current work as well as projected feelings about leaving your work.

Think over the following questions; depending on your responses, you may be ready to leave the formal working aspects of your life behind:

- Is your current work boring? Stressful?
- Are work demands changing? Can you keep up? Do you want to?
- Are you healthy enough to do your work well? Will you be able to continue, physically, over the next several years?
- Is your earning power flat? Are your efforts unrewarded? No promotions in sight?
- Have you been offered a buyout? Can you afford to take it? What are the consequences if you refuse?
- Are you being forced out by a reduction-in-force (RIF)? What's in your immediate future?
- What's your tentative conclusion? Would it be better to get out now?

If you are in a stressful situation in your job and can retire without causing more stress than what you have while working, RETIRE!

—Anthony, age 55, retired at age 50

Changes were being made in the unit in which I worked, and my boss decided that I would be required to work different time schedules. It was then that I decided to retire. I do miss seeing my friends, although some of us still meet for lunch or evening dinner occasionally. I manage to fill my days with family, friends, church, women's clubs, and volunteer work. Although my retirement check is very small, I am grateful each month to receive it.

—Nell, age 70, retired at age 60

I retired a couple of years "early" because of moderate job dissatisfaction and adequate retirement income. These have definitely been the best years of my life. Very important factors are excellent health, fine home, rewarding community activities, intellectual pursuits, good friends, a sense of continuing personal development, fine relationships with adult children and their families.

The chief problem is that I find more desirable interests and activities than I can follow. Best advice to pre-retirees: Plan ahead!

—Jason, age 72, retired at age 63

I took retirement at age 50. I think 30 years in the work force is long enough. I started thinking retirement around 20 years of age. Instead of spending my bonus checks, I decided to buy different stock each year.

—Cal, age 59, retired at age 50

The best part of retirement is the pressure that I was under is gone. The worst was leaving the people I worked around for years.

—Carl, age 56, retired at age 52

I miss the people, but love the freedom of not having to go to work every day.

—Arne, age 53, retired at age 52

Leave as soon as you can.

—Al, age 56, retired at age 55

If a person's identity is strongly connected to their job, they will need to make significant adjustments in retirement.

—Bob, age 55, retired at age 55

I could have worked much longer, but I am very happy retired. I'm sure many workers stay on their jobs too long.

—Vera, age 70, retired at age 59

When I retired, my first concern was that "I was over the hill," and it took a couple of years before I thoroughly adjusted. I even became concerned about my health. I found it difficult to "let go" and really relax from the previous day-to-day pressures. As I assumed more activities in my retirement that I felt were worthy and significant, my former position became less and less important.

—Faith, age 72, retired at age 60

There is life beyond work years.

—Rachael, age 66, retired at age 62

My biggest surprise was how quickly I lost interest in my work, which I enjoyed very much prior to retirement.

—Jack, age 65, retired at age 62

Advice: retire as soon as possible, as the retirement years pass quicker than you can ever foresee.

—Joe, age 79, retired at age 62

The thing I miss related to my employment is that fine group of people I worked with.

—Rob, age 68, retired at age 63

Bad things about retirement:
1. Floundering to replace main thrust of my life.
2. Feeling of loss of identity.
3. Loss of reason for being.
4. Diminished self-image.
5. Fewer bucks (not as serious as above effects).

—Harvey, age 69, retired at age 63

Those Who Stay

My college roommate, now age 80, has said to me repeatedly, "I'm never going to retire." His adage: The Best Never Rest! He's great in technical sales and public relations and may well keep working for another decade or more. Eventually, some of the same forces which shape early retirement will enter his life, too.

For now, however, there is a much different set of forces driving his working life. These concepts have been expressed by the 30% of current retirees who report some unhappiness about leaving their jobs, whether it was early or late in their working life.

Work through the following questions. If you answer most of these positively, you are a great candidate to keep working beyond the "normal" retirement date:

- Do you enjoy the discipline and routine of work? Schedules, deadlines, shifts?
- Do you adapt easily to changes in the work environment? Personnel changes, computer systems, management policies?
- Will you miss socializing with your co-workers? Helping them through work as well as personal crises?
- Are you a highly motivated workaholic? Can you slow down? Relax? Do you really want your freedom?
- Are you likely to experience a personal loss of self-esteem and identity if you leave your work? What will happen when the power is gone?

One retiree, Alex, currently age 60 but retired at age 55, got to the point in a hurry. When asked to comment about retirement, he offered a singular response: "Don't…"

> Retirement was the worst thing that could have happened to me, except losing my health. I'm currently working two jobs. My wife works also.
>
> —Abner, age 55, retired at age 50

> For a brief six months I was totally lost! My work had been my life. Soon thereafter, I was able to re-establish my industrial consulting practice. It became, for all practical purposes, a full-time job that I continued until I prepared consulting report #137. All of this was discontinued when I became ill with a virus and spent two months "bedfast." Since that time (six years ago) I have deteriorated. Further complications included a stroke by my wife. Advice to pre-retirees: Prepare yourself for interesting work during your retirement. It will prevent you from "going nuts"!
>
> —Dave, age 89, retired at age 66

> When I first retired, I thought retirement was "just a piece of cake"! However, in about a month I'd completed all the tasks one doesn't do when time is limited. I found that I was pretty much alone, inasmuch as my husband had died about 10 years before I retired. I soon began missing work and the people with whom I'd worked. My solution was to go back to work part-time for four days per week. I kept that job for four years, making my employment total 41 years.
>
> —Alma, age 84, retired at age 66

> The day they said I could not work was the worst day of my life. I had a heart attack and they said I couldn't work any more.
>
> —Rich, age 73, retired at age 63

> I found I wanted to go back to work. I missed the routine of daily work, missed the people I worked with, and missed patient care. One year after retiring I took a job as RN at a large clinic

in Urgent Care and still work there. I love the work, the patients, and the companionship of the other nurses. So for the past nine years I've worked and hope to work many more. I believe if you enjoy your job, try to find a part-time job in your field or stay in the job you have.

—Melanie, age 74, retired at age 65

I believe working is therapy; work as long as you can. To stop work is to begin the death process. The same applies to learning and socializing.

—Stan, age 68, retired at age 68

Had an easy job, loved it, loved the people, should have stayed on for 10 years more because I am bored with extra time on my hands. Now I'm working part-time on three different jobs.

—Jerome, age 72, retired at age 65

I worked as a chief executive officer of a 5,000-member professional organization for four years after retirement and currently work as a professional witness.

—Guthrie, age 79, retired at age 70

If your job is stressful, like mine was, find another one less stressful to finish your years out. I wish I had, instead of leaving completely, but I needed the rest.

—Mary, age 61, retired at age 56

The best is that I have been working part-time after retirement. I could name my hours and time I wanted to work. So please stay as long as you can or your health will let you. Because the longer you work, the more retirement income you will receive.

—Cheryl, age 68, retired at age 66

Never retire before reaching age 65 or 70. If your health is good, you have plenty of time to enjoy things. Invest the max in your savings plan.

—Jim, age 74, retired at age 65

I retired too early and had too many bills to live on a retirement check roughly one-half of my normal pay. I had to take a new job at one-half of my pre-retirement check. This year I had prostate cancer and was operated on. I still have to work after cancer.

—Don, age 55, retired at age 50

Work after Retirement?

A part-time job? A new career? Bored, need the cash, or ready to scale your personal Mount Everest? Whatever your reasons and your preferences, retirees are taking on new and vigorous work roles.

If they work at all, retirees typically work part-time. They have a national reputation for being dependable, and they are especially sensitive to the need for excellent customer service. Younger employees often learn much about patience, good service, and hard work from those with a lifetime of experience.

At one extreme, your retirement income simply won't pay the bills. You need a job. At the other extreme, you are flunking retirement. You are bored. You need a new challenge for your talents and your pent-up energy. At least, this is what you think you need.

Workaholics are addicted to work, but not necessarily to jobs. They can be creative mentors and teachers, consultants, and entrepreneurs. Often family continues to rank second in importance to their work.

In any case, find your new niche soon after retirement. You may need to work 10 to 20 hours per week in a local hardware store or lumber yard. Perhaps a travel agency or a mall shop? Alternately, your new career may involve raising venture capital for new biomedical products.

If you don't need to work, use your time and energy to help others. If you miss your job and want to help other retirees, volunteer to work for the retiree organization to which you may already belong. Give a few hours every week to your local community center or crisis center. Your church and its youth clubs, perhaps a local school or reading academy, a hospital: they need you!

Chase a few bucks or make a million. What matters equally is how you engage your mind and your body in meaningful activities. If you walk away from your job, you will have 30, 40, or 50 hours per week of new time. What creative activity will fill that void? Do you have a clue?

My Personal Space: Early, Now, or Never

List two or more of the most important reasons you should retire.

List two or more of the most important reasons you should put off retirement and keep working. Discuss both lists with your spouse or significant other in order to avoid any surprises.

What is your current work week—30, 40, 50 hours? When you retire, what will you do with these hours? Do you have some short-term goals, such as painting the house or cleaning the basement? What long-term goals should you consider? What does your family say about your goals?

WORK: WHAT SOME RETIREES SAY...

I was surprised to find I was slightly down and depressed for the first several months. I found traveling helped me. I needed to wind down after the frantic pace kept at work. I miss the people I worked with very much. I visit the office when I can. The only advice I have is to not be surprised if you react differently than you planned when you first retire.

—Shirley, age 65, retired at age 65

The first two months I was very restless. Cleaned with a fury, painted, wallpapered, etc. These new activities resulted in a bad case of sciatica—spent the next six months recovering! Since then have been volunteering at a local agency for 15 hours a week, which keeps me sane. All in all it was a slow, gradual adjustment, and now I feel back in a groove—a more relaxed groove—but it's OK. The freedom is enjoyable!

—Alice, age 67, retired at age 65

The best: freedom from office politics; decisions rendered inconsistently and non-uniformly; superficial evaluations and special cases. The worst: insider-to-outsider with no transition period for adjustment.

—Kent, age 69, retired at age 66

I suggest to younger colleagues that they be a little less work-centered and a little more family-centered while still working. The rewards will be much longer lasting.

—Frank, age 73, retired at age 70

I found initially that I missed the socialization of the workplace. Developing and maintaining relationships is hard work in retirement; it was easy at work. This may be obvious, but it is the toughest to replace.

—Jim, age 67, retired at age 65

Frankly, I don't miss my departmental colleagues because there never was much sense of community there. I found friendships elsewhere.

—Justin, age 69, retired at age 65

On retirement, I left the world of work-related pressures, of committee meetings, reports, deadlines, and I started a new life of freedom to use my time as I wished. The change in lifestyle was of course pleasurable, and I took full advantage of my freedom to travel and catch up on reading for pleasure. However, life with lots of time soon became boring and frustrating. It is difficult to go from a life where you had professional challenges to one where you have to invent "jobs" to perform to gain satisfaction. I find that I miss the fun of solving problems and generally enjoying the everyday routines of a job.

My advice from the experience of retirement for seven years is to do the following:

1. Take partial retirement and slowly phase out of your job.
2. Plan to do volunteer work and to keep to a "work schedule."
3. At home take up new hobbies and activities which provide a new challenge.

I have spent my time using the computer and experimenting with new software. I became serious with my interest in photography and a camcorder, and now I have expanded these interests with digital photography and editing of videos.

—Bill, age 72, retired at age 65

It's my opinion that the majority of people work too long. They are too old when they retire. Their retirement years are filled with health problems and inability to travel because of poor physical/ mental health.

—Louis, age 60, retired at age 60

I find my responsibilities at home utilize many skills I learned during my employment. I did experience "technology with- drawal" and had to purchase a copier and a fax! One sugges- tion: It seems to me that many retirees would be interested in continuing their technology education. For example, one may wish to improve computer Internet skills. This may be particu- larly true with recent and future retirees, who are more oriented to computers.

—Janice, age 51, retired at age 50

We both enjoyed working, and our positions at our place of em- ployment were very fulfilling. Our retirement is now the same.

—Lissa, age 64, retired at age 61

I had a hobby that was getting out of hand, and it was much more fun than my job, so I retired to do it full time. I get a modest in- come from it, but I don't work at it like I did my job. If I want the day off, I take it! It's been wonderful!

—Joanne, age 65, retired at age 62

The worst: not having a secretary.

—Dwight, age 72, retired at age 65

I had never planned to take an early retirement—I wanted to go on as long as possible. Fortunately, I have not retired and am still engaged in work I find useful and productive. Without this,

I would have become insane. Thus, from my viewpoint, another type of work (at least another type of activity) is essential. My biggest advice to potential retirees, especially those contemplating early retirement, would be to ease into it—to have another "job" in mind—not just in mind, but actually arranged.

> —Millie, age 66, retired at age 55

If your work brings you satisfaction, then work. If not, then find what does. Whether it's employment or retirement, you'll know.

> —Clyde, age 67, retired at age 60

I loved my work, and I miss it. I hated my job, and I do not miss it.

> —Mac, age 53, retired at age 52

I retired from a job to a career. My income increased, my anxiety level decreased, my church and community involvement increased. I may retire from my career in 15 to 20 years, maybe not. It's too much fun to think about.

> —Jim, age 51, retired at age 51

You may soon experience how unimportant one becomes upon retirement. I hope not.

> —Alex, age 67, retired at age 63

Chapter 6

Ties That Bind

- I do not want to move away from my family and friends.
- I am considering relocation to a different community.
- I plan to reside permanently in my current community.
- I would like to own a vacation home in a different climate.
- My parents are not a burden to me.
- Religious activities are an important part of my life.

Relocate? Stay put? Buy a small vacation home for summers or winters? Downsize but stay local? Easy questions, often tough to answer.

In an AARP national study, over four out of five retirees (83%) say they would prefer to stay put. They like their home and its proximity to family, friends, and amenities—shopping, restaurants, churches, libraries, health clubs, the arts.

Another group is restless, perhaps adventuresome. They need to relocate, often within the same year that they retire. There is no right or wrong, but there are reasons on both sides of the question.

This domain, Family and Friends, might be viewed simply as "relocation," but it is more complex, as you will see.

First, in my survey of 700 retirees, 84% expressed positive feelings about staying in their current community after retirement. Only 10% expressed dissatisfaction, but, in fact, 20% eventually will move to a new state after retirement.

Most retirees have family ties in their hometown. If their children have moved away, they still have a network of close friends, some going back to early childhood. Simply put, they don't want to leave their comfortable circumstances.

Other retirees cannot leave. Some cannot afford to uproot. Others are caregivers for their aging parents or grandchildren. One spouse or the other may have a life-threatening disease. Moving is out of the question; local support networks couldn't be replicated easily.

> Keeping busy, maintaining your health through exercise and nutrition, and being near family are the most important ways to be happy.
>
> —Judy, age 82, retired at age 64

> My wife discovered she had cancer a week after she took retirement. Even though doctors claimed after surgery and chemotherapy that "they got it all," the cancer came back three years later and took her life.
>
> We enjoyed those three years together very much. In order to do so, I took early retirement and we traveled, spent time with our children and grandchildren. She encouraged me to remarry after she died.
>
> Life goes on, and I continue to plan for the future. I try to enjoy each day to the fullest.
>
> —Ray, age 72, retired at age 62

> I retired early to care for my invalid husband who lived another five years. Those years were very hard and physically draining, but after his death I became involved in several organizations, traveled a little, resumed old friendships, and volunteered where I could. While my plans aren't rigid, I do plan something to do every day.
>
> —Janet, age 73, retired at age 63

> I loved my job and would have worked longer but my mother lived with my husband and me, and I was her sole caregiver. We have no children, and our relatives live on the East or West coast. When she was 95, it was necessary for her to live in a nursing home. She died at the age of 100, two years ago. Now we don't have the enthusiasm we had then—but we have developed other interests and always find new pastimes. The one fear is not hav-

ing money to be cared for if one of us would be disabled or an invalid (especially after one of us dies).

—Carole, age 68, retired at age 61

My wife and I remain in our own home, in a neighborhood and community in which we are comfortable. Although our children live out West, we are able to make vacations of our visits. We have traveled on our own and with groups that share our interests in hiking, geology, and botany to New Zealand, Hawaii, the Grand Canyon, Iceland, and Great Britain. All of this has been made possible by regular, prudent, long-term savings and investment. Staying on after 65 produced such an increase in income that I made more by retiring than continuing further work.

—Milt, age 75, retired at age 69

My husband died six years ago—after a year's illness. After five years of living alone and being content to be alone, I chose to reside in a local retirement community. It's a good place for me at this point—complete freedom of movement and activities, but the complexities of keeping up a home are minimized.

—Judy, age 80, retired at age 63

My situation is better understood by knowing that my wife is handicapped by multiple sclerosis. At the time of my retirement, she was functioning in a two-story house with a cane and a walker. Gradually, a wheelchair became necessary as walking became more difficult. Eventually, she could no longer handle the upper floor at home nor travel comfortably out of town. At that time we built an addition to the house to provide a bedroom and complete bath on the first floor.

—Bradley, age 77, retired at age 65

We spent three years before we retired looking around, and I would suggest this to anyone. Before you retire or make a move, spend time with a planner to see if you think you can do it. Moving to another state is not cheap and is a real adjustment.

—Miles, age 54, retired at age 53

Climate, recreation, downsizing, and health are cited regularly as the principal reasons that retirees move. Each family has unique circumstances: cheaper cost-of-living, a new business opportunity, the need to become a caregiver. Other families find that their children have moved away, and their local ties are tenuous. Still others are loners with no apparent ties at all.

There is a principle which applies to the Family and Friends domain: **Relocate only if you have good reasons. Before you move, explore alternate locations, lifestyles, and costs.**

Two alternatives: a vacation getaway or a smaller home in your own community.

What does vacation mean to you? Big city hotels, RV camping, a fishing lodge, a Florida condominium to rent by the week or the season? An alternative is the vacation home, a second home, or condominium you purchase for your periodic use. Summer fun or winter sports? Drive an hour or two or fly several hours to get there? The same principle applies here as it does to relocation. Buy only if you have good reasons: to enjoy family and friends, climate, and lifestyle, perhaps even the gain on your investment. But beware that a second home often requires upgrades and maintenance which can sap your emotional strength and your wallet. This is a vacation?

Most retirees don't need to downsize right away—that comes later in life. But some want fewer responsibilities for lawns and leaky roofs, fresh paint, and furnace replacements.

Downsize if you have the stamina. Upsize if you are loaded. Who doesn't know a retiree who decides to build a dream home at age 55 or 65—with 5,500 or 6,500 square feet or much more? Great for some, nuts for others!

The Retired and the Restless

This group of retirees comes in two flavors: itchy, hell-bent to move, and the careful planners. Whatever their reasons, they move.

You have seen the come-ons in many "leisure" ads and publications:

- A lifestyle that lasts a lifetime…Sun, blue skies, gentle breezes…Shopping, beaches, cultural events, restaurants to suit every palate…
- Lifestyles you have come to expect…Dances, arts and crafts, cards, billiards…Clubhouse overlooking a well-stocked lake…Championship golf nearby…
- A lifestyle of catered elegance…Luxurious, affordable, and fun…Conveniently located within walking distance of churches, banks, post office, shopping…Exciting floor plans, 24-hour security, housekeeping, scheduled transportation, and amenities galore!

Add in your own personal requirements: skiing at Snomass or Stowe; fishing in the Columbia River; the symphony, ballet, or a community theatre—add them in only if they are lifestyle demands based on your track record at home, not your immediate whim for the future.

If you have kept to the principle of this domain, if you have good reasons to move, if you have explored alternatives carefully *and* you are satisfied with your answers, then do it!

> We moved out of state to a new community that necessitated making new friends and associates. Our home is very comfortable in an area of increasing values, and the area is considered to be a vacationland. Retirement is great and I recommend it!
>
> —Harry, age 72, retired at age 67

> Retirement had not brought about any dramatic changes in our lifestyle even though we moved to a warmer climate eight years ago. We miss being close to our children and their families. We miss the change of seasons and are not sure that we should have completely given up our home. Perhaps a part-year move to a smaller home would have been a better choice.
>
> —Jordan, age 78, retired at age 63

Free advice:

    1) Plan for retirement financially.

    2) Move away from family and friends, but keep all of

them in your life. Retirement is a time for you as an individual. Take no baggage (family, hang-ups, etc.). Meet new people, make new friends, go places you enjoy, do things you enjoy.

3) Become active with church, organizations, clubs that are your choice.

4) Stay healthy; without it you cannot enjoy any of the above.

5) Be happy, don't think "what if." Live for today.

—Judy, age 61, retired at age 60

I moved to Florida, but was away from family, so moved back home to Indiana.

—Kemper, age 64, retired at age 51

I moved immediately after retirement. I had looked for a location for the previous six years, love it, have never missed work or people, have new friends. I set parameters I wanted, then went looking: 1) climate, 2) view of mountains, 3) near metropolitan area and airport, 4) land with home, 5) sunsets, 6) big sky, 7) seasons, but not much snow.

—Pat, age 62, retired at age 57

I relocated to a community with other retirees. It is an area of good fishing, which is my main enjoyment, and the climate is warmer. The best advice I can give is plan, plan, plan and early. I love retirement. It is the highlight of my life.

—Jay, age 56, retired at age 54

We prepared to relocate for at least three years. Then we moved to Arizona and built a house.

We go to Laughlin or Las Vegas at least once per month for cheap food and good entertainment. We wake up every morning with sunshine and a grand view of three different mountain ranges. We can see snow from our patio and that's close enough.

Free advice:

1) Start three to four years before retirement and get fi-

nances in order. Waiting won't get it!

2) Buy land/property before retiring and have it paid for—both residence and all improvements. Be sure to travel to several places and spend some time to see how things operate— allergies, special needs, etc. —before deciding to move.

3) Local medical treatment is very important when relocating—check it out.

4) This is your time to enjoy. If you made your job your life, you will shortchange your retirement. If you enjoy and pursue your hobbies, you'll never have to work again.

—Dave, age 58, retired at age 53

Over-55 Retirement Communities

If a retirement community is the right place for you, consider how to protect your independent lifestyle in future years. Is there a clubhouse, a social program, a golf course, an exercise room? Is there an assisted living facility (ALF) or a medical clinic on the premises? What home health agencies are located nearby? Hospitals? Surely you don't need any of these services now, but you may.

Is your investment secure? Will it increase in value with good resale prospects? Have monthly maintenance fees remained stable? Need earthquake or flood insurance? Liability insurance, if you rent your property occasionally? This list never seems to end.

We're Home, Toto!

Do you recall Dorothy's famous line near the end of *The Wizard of Oz*? For most retirees, home equates to family and friends, to a safe harbor, and often to years of spirited fun and loving memories.

My own parents moved from Chicago to St. Petersburg, Florida, when they were in their early 60s. They had their reasons: health, cost of living, climate. Their focus had been on family and now they felt isolated. Their brand new house was not really their home.

The bottom line on moving focuses on family first, friends next, and then community ties. If there are other reasons to move, they should be more compelling than family and friends. These are truly the ties that bind.

My Personal Space: Ties That Bind

What are the most important reasons you should move? Immediately after retirement? Within five years? Where?

What are the most important reasons you should not relocate after retirement? Health? Finances? Family?

What relocation costs might you incur?

> *Housing. Can you afford to rent or buy? Downsize?*
>
> *Moving. Who will pack? Who will pay?*
>
> *Taxes. Increased or decreased income, real estate, sales,*
> *intangibles, estate, and inheritance taxes?*

Have you considered climate, recreation, transportation? When will you see your family?

FAMILY AND FRIENDS: WHAT SOME RETIREES SAY...

Good food, good friends, good family relations make for "good living."

—John, age 68, retired at age 64

When I retired, I was not ready for retirement. I felt like I was just "getting on a roll" and enjoyed my work even though it was stressful at times. I missed my job and co-workers so much that I visited the office every week for the first two years. My wife and I have been caregivers for her mother for almost six years. This has prevented us from taking any vacations except for a day or two. This has been more stressful than we could have imagined.

—Hugh, age 65, retired at age 61

Don't retire too early. If you have children at home or in school, it restricts you so much that you tend to blame it on retirement.

—Harley, age 58, retired at age 52

The worst thing that has happened is that our eldest child is presently going through a divorce, and the spouse has charge of all money matters. They are deep in debt, and he could not even afford a lawyer. I had not planned for anything like this.

—Holden, age 64, retired at age 59

My retirement has overall been a good experience. I have been able to keep active in my favorite hobby—music. My four children and eight grandchildren have been a constant joy, with none of them giving me any cause to worry other than the normal minor problems of any family. I've had two things occur that were sad and discouraging: major heart surgery three years ago and the death of my wife last year. I feel I've been able to adjust to these adversities fairly well. I just take life one day at a time, and thank God for each new morning. That's the advice I would give anyone considering retirement.

—Bernie, age 70, retired at age 61

I retired at age 52 to take care of my mother. I am an only child, and my mother was in the final stages of lymphoma. After my mother's death, I felt I was too young to retire completely, so I started a business of my own.

—Perry, age 62, retired at age 52

I had planned to retire at 65, not 58. I was not prepared mentally, and I thought I was not prepared financially. I worked part-time for one year and then full time for one year before I completely retired. At that point I was mentally ready to retire. Another big change was marriage after one year of retirement. That has made retirement even better and more enjoyable for both of us. My advice would be to start saving early in life. Don't depend on anyone else completely.

—Becky, age 63, retired at age 58

I am enjoying retirement more than I thought I would in the beginning. It was difficult for me to get used to. My husband passed away just before I retired and that didn't help. I had worked for 45 years. I missed the people I worked with, and I missed my job. It took me about a year to get used to being retired.

—Ethel, age 69, retired at age 63

Chapter 7

To Your Health!

- I worry about having health problems.
- I am fearful of getting cancer.
- Depression has been a problem for me.
- My weight has increased in recent years.
- I balance diet and exercise to keep my weight under control.
- Regular exercise keeps me fit.
- I enjoy good health.
- I am optimistic about the future.

Do you remember *Everything You Always Wanted to Know About Sex (but Were Afraid to Ask)*? As a teen, you probably inhaled every word, every page. Not much communication with mom and dad? They kept their feelings about sex to themselves. Well, there are other topics mom and dad were silent about as well—their pre- and post-retirement years and the accompanying changes in their health.

You are facing those same years, those same transitions from work to retirement. Some aspects of the health environment have changed dramatically in recent decades. In the 1970s, 46% of Americans were overweight; now the figure is 64% and rising. We expect our physicians to cure nearly everything with a pill—and with one that works instantly!

The leading causes of death in both men and women continue to be heart disease, cancer, and stroke, but death seems an eternity away. Death visits older retirees, not younger ones, especially not those just thinking about their retirement.

If you could get some recent retirees to "open up" about their health changes, their litany would sound like this:

- My joints aren't so limber any more.
- My blood pressure is up a bit.
- I am a little forgetful at times.
- My bruises don't heal up very fast. My fingernails break easily.
- Sometimes I have a little trouble breathing.
- I just don't have the energy I used to have; I tire easily.
- I am a few pounds heavier than when I retired.

Generalities, every one. Yes, most are all too true, and, taken three or four at a time, they can lead to a poor quality of life at an early age. But these changes beg the real transitions that occur around the typical retirement years.

Of all the retirees I have surveyed and interviewed, 68% enjoy reasonably good health, and 21% report moderate-to-severe health problems. Do these attitudes derive from minor aches and pains, stiff joints, lack of energy, and a few extra pounds? No. This current generation of retirees is nearly as tight-lipped as your parents and grandparents. But there are a few retirees who are willing to open up; they tell an incredible story that you have never heard before.

Here gender prevails, and there are significant differences in the general health transitions for male retirees and for female retirees. Each gender needs to read through both stories in order to understand the whole health picture.

The Male Angle: PHAD

Say "fad." Go ahead, say it out loud, "fad."

The letters stand for ordinary terms we use in our daily lives; these terms often mark the series of transitions which occur as we move from work to retirement:

P = Power
P = Prostate
P = Penis
H = Health
A = Anxiety
D = Depression

The First P

A short feature in *Newsweek* asked the rhetorical question, "What Is It Like When the Power Is Gone?" While the definition of power varies, feelings about power are very consistent.

What type of a job do you have? Are you the vice president of a Fortune 1,000 company? A manager? A clerk-typist? Perhaps you are simply "the boss," the owner of your own company.

First of all, you enjoy the feel of power. Perhaps you budget and oversee 5,000 employees in a sector of a large manufacturing corporation; perhaps you are a department manager with a staff of 100, or you supervise one or two temps on a part-time basis. Beyond power, you enjoy authority, even control. In every case, work is dished out by those in charge, and everyone understands the pecking order.

When the power terminates, when the flow of information is curtailed, when your salary is reduced, new feelings emerge: loss of power, inadequacy, rejection, failure. This is the first of the retirement switches to trip, for males and females alike. Simply stated, this loss of power—the first P—is felt by every retiree. The degree varies depending on the extent of responsibility and personal identification the retiree has with their work, but the impact is there for everyone. Even denial won't negate your feelings—your losses—for long.

More P

Add to this loss of ego another change, this time a physical change. Benign Prostatic Hyperplasia (BPH), noncancerous enlargement of the prostate gland, occurs in 50% of all men over the age of 50 and 80% of all men over the age of 80.

The prostate gland is a walnut-sized gland located directly under the male bladder. As men age, the prostate enlarges and muscles within it tighten. Difficulty with urination may creep in or occur suddenly.

Tell-tale signs show up over a few months to a few years, typically sooner. The symptoms of BPH are easy to spot:

- Need to urinate often, especially at night
- Urgency to urinate
- Inability to empty the bladder

- Weak stream with some stopping and starting
- Weak start, sometimes with pushing or straining to begin.

When the first two or three symptoms become noticeable, you have to urinate at intervals much less than two hours. Sometimes the urgency is so great that you do not quite make it to the urinal in time. Alternately, you may have been in a public restroom with several older males. Quite often, they just stand at their urinals, hoping.

BPH also is the major cause of urgent trips to the bathroom in the middle of the night. You know that if you drink much coffee or beer before bedtime, you will have to get up to urinate. If you watch your intake and still get up twice every night (or even three or four times) you are certainly a candidate for BPH. Annoying, yes; bothersome, absolutely; deadly, probably not, but it is absolutely necessary to discuss this with your physician.

Tell my physician about what? Let's hope he never asks me about any of this, because there might be more to the story. Most men feel vulnerable and threatened if their physician asks about their prostate—read personal—problems.

But help is available for the brave ones. Your physician may suggest "watchful waiting" or may prescribe a drug such as Hytrin, Cardura, or Flomax. These cause smooth muscles in the prostate and the neck of the bladder to relax. This, in turn, increases the urinary flow rate and decreases the symptoms of BPH. Hytrin and Cardura also are used to reduce hypertension. Side effects for all three vary but sometimes include dizziness, headache, fatigue, and impotence or other sexual dysfunction.

An alternative remedy is saw palmetto, which can be purchased over the counter in most drug stores as well as in nutrition and health food stores. One or two pills per day of saw palmetto from a reliable manufacturer normally will bring visible relief within one-to-two weeks and without known side effects. And no, what you really wanted to know but were afraid to ask, saw palmetto will not interfere with your erections.

Unfortunately, the prostate gland sometimes requires surgery, either for extreme prostate enlargement or for prostate cancer. Your friendly physician will do a digital rectal examination (DRE) at least annually, a prostate-specific antigen (PSA) blood test for cancer screening, and quite possibly a biopsy of prostate tissue if there is any suspicion of cancer.

All of this male talk about the P—the prostate—upsets the male psyche. Your power is gone, your prostate is enlarged, what's next? As if you didn't know…

Another P

Another major transition which occurs in males around the time of retirement is diminished sexual ability. Call it aging, over-the-hill, tired blood, or whatever, it is the third of the male nightmares. According to the Massachusetts Male Aging Study (MMAS), approximately 50% of 60-year-old men have moderate problems getting or maintaining erections. And this represents only the men who are willing to discuss and admit to their concerns.

Impotence, the inability to achieve or to maintain an erection, is devastating to men and their partners. Both psychological and physical components are present. Self-image and self-esteem self-destruct when men no longer get erections. Relationships falter and sometimes are destroyed when sexual intercourse is impossible due to impotence.

Male testosterone production peaks, on average, around age 20 to 25 years, not at all around age 40 (like you thought). Luckily, your production system is somewhat overdesigned: you're at 60% of your peak at age 50, 40% of your peak at age 60, and continuing on the downhill slope.

While the term "impotence" has been around for decades, the new medical term is erectile dysfunction or "ED." There may be some psychological factors, such as death of a partner, lack of availability of a partner, failed relationships (often hostility or doubt about your partner), and vocational failure. This perceived failure is where feelings about the loss of power creep in. For some, retirement is an implied vocational failure, even if the male has had many years of success in business or in a profession. Feelings of despair, uncertainty, guilt, and even unworthiness are part of the retirement transitions that show up in the bedroom.

Luckily, the principal causes of ED are organic; unluckily, the medical reasons are varied and thus so are the potential remedies. Atherosclerosis, the deposit of fatty plaque in the small arteries of the penis, is a leading cause of ED. Abnormal venous drainage or "leaks" also result in ED. Both of these are compounded by aging, surgical trauma, and specific diseases, such as diabetes, thyroid dysfunction, and kidney failure.

Most of all, medication is likely to be the most common cause of ED. Two classes of drugs that are often implicated are the antihypertensives and the antidepressant compounds. Tranquilizers reportedly decrease libido, as do large concentrations of alcohol.

Treatments of ED are as varied as the causes. The main difficulty is that you cannot quite distinguish the treat from the treatment.

Imagine a vacuum pump device which removes air from a cylinder fitted around your penis. The decreased pressure promotes blood flow into the penis, and the erection is maintained by a tight rubber ring rolled down about the base of your penis. I am told it works.

A second method is to inject a smooth muscle relaxant, usually coupled with vasodilators, directly into the base of your penis. A normal erection follows within 10 to 20 minutes and can easily last an hour. I am assured that this technique works, but I am squeamish and have not tried it.

Several types of penile implants are available. The most common is a flexible rod that can be permanently implanted in your penis. This offers a rather bold look as well as enough rigidity for sex. I passed on this procedure, too.

The best of the methodologies seems to me to be Viagra, Levitra, and Cialis (and succeeding generations of similar oral drugs). A single tablet taken about an hour before sexual activity normally will result in a strong erection. Some stimulation may be needed. One current drawback is the 45 minute (or longer) wait for Viagra to be absorbed in the body. A good friend of mine jokes that Viagra also promotes good communications; surely, you or your spouse has said to the other, "Dinner will be ready in about 45 minutes."

H Stands for Health

Male health concerns span a broad range of problems, both organic and psychological in nature. If present, these are the fourth major factor that leads to health transitions around the time of retirement. Only a few specific illustrations will be presented; as you might expect, the range of medical possibilities is enormous.

Some health factors are inevitable (or so it seems): your hairline has receded, perhaps even showing a male baldness pattern; your waist was once a 30 or 32 and now it is a full 36 or 38 inches, maybe larger. Well, neither of those has much to do with transitions around the time of retirement. Others do. The following health changes frequently impact men shortly before or after their retirement:

- High blood pressure. May lead to hypertension and one of several heart diseases.
- High cholesterol. Often leads to heart disease, such as myocardial infarction (heart attack).
- Obesity. Unusual overload on the heart as well as on the body at large.
- Colorectal cancer. Have you done your occult blood test this year? Sigmoidoscopy?
- Smoking. Those who have not stopped are candidates for emphysema, if not lung cancer and death.
- Alcoholism. Ask your physician to explain liver damage and what is likely to follow. Then quit drinking or cut way back!

We will leave out genital warts, STDs, and AIDS. If you have not been messing around, there is no reason to start at retirement age.

But you may be vulnerable to other health transitions around age 55 or older. Your parents may be aging and need considerable health care. Many of them will die around the time you retire, either before or after. Your spouse or partner may become ill with a disease that limits your ability to travel or requires an enormous amount of your care. Or your spouse may die. Any of these changes will affect you psychologically every bit as much as if you developed a major health problem yourself.

Next?

That depends on the P's and the H's in your life. If you have experienced one or two of these transitions, you are a potential candidate to continue further into PHAD. If you have experienced many of these transitions in a serious way, you are likely to move further along into the PHAD sequence. But first, let us see what health concerns men are willing to discuss openly.

WHAT MEN ARE WILLING TO DISCUSS ABOUT HEALTH...

The worst things about retirement are declining health (or fear of it), higher out-of-pocket costs for health/long-term care and life insurance, loss of involvement in community projects, and seeing former associates move away or pass on.

—Jack, age 68, retired at age 62

The main things for a happy retirement: health, sufficient finances, and attitude.

—Chet, age 63, retired at age 62

Don't spend half of your life looking at a computer screen—get some exercise!

—Rob, age 76, retired at age 66

The best of our retirement has been our tours of foreign countries and time with our grandchildren. The worst of our retirement has been three major surgeries, including prostate cancer. Advice to those considering retirement: to have as good health as can be achieved and to have as much money as can be accumulated without being a miser.

—Richard, age 68, retired at age 64

Metamucil? Denture cream? No way, man!

—Dick, age 68, retired at age 62

Our major concerns have been health problems. My wife has severe sight and voice problems, and I have had heart problems (quadruple by-pass surgery). Health insurance and medical paperwork are somewhat confusing and should be simplified.

—Lanny, age 68, retired at age 60

The best part of my retirement is that my health has improved because of less stress. I enjoy the freedom of not having to show up at the plant and not having to work on Sundays. The biggest surprise to me is that I do not miss my co-workers as much as I thought I would. I guess that since I am with my family more, that takes the place of my co-workers. I really enjoy retirement and do not miss a thing about my former workplace.

—Lindley, age 55, retired at age 54

I started my own woodworking business. I didn't know how good I felt until after retirement.

—Jake, age 56, retired at age 55

Biggest surprise: the amount of job pressure that I did not know was there. My headaches stopped, and I am more relaxed.

—Blair, age 62, retired at age 57

I have enjoyed my retirement from day one. The best thing has been an almost 100% reduction in stress. This has resulted in "a better night's sleep" and being much easier to live with. Equally important is the opportunity to go to daily mass.

It takes three things to have a good retirement:
1) Retiree's good health
2) Spouse's good health
3) Sufficient income

—Willard, age 69, retired at age 58

The first fifteen months of retirement were great. Then I had a quadruple coronary bypass. I had my abdominal aorta removed and laced with an artificial aorta. Since then it's been fighting heart problems. I have been in cardiac rehab since 1991.

—Keith, age 80, retired at age 70

In January, after retiring in December, I had open heart surgery. This was my worst. While in the hospital recovering, we had our first grandson. This was my best. I attend rehab three days a week to stay in shape, and I am able to do almost everything I did before heart surgery. Retirement has been very good to us; we go as we please and do things as we wish.

—Douglas, age 66, retired at age 62

The last day of my employment, my wife became violently ill, spent two months in hospital, had major and crippling surgery, and had limited recovery. Moral: Don't hold off on your plans to travel until you retire. Do it when you are physically competent.

Find activities in which you can make meaningful contributions in retirement. Most of my present friends I have met since I retired.

You don't need a lot of money. I asked one older friend who lives in a retirement community what he does now. He said: "I sit here and accumulate."

I divide retirees into three groups:

a) The 60s and 70s: still physically and mentally alert. How wonderful to be ladies and gentlemen of leisure.

b) The 80s: the ailing. Health problems rule and limit. If you can still see and hear, you are lucky.

c) The old: in nursing homes. We are sorry for them and dread the day we join them, but even there, for some it is still *Carpe Diem*. Bless them.

— Raymond, age 84, retired at age 68

My wife is in the beginning stages of Alzheimer's. Our future is very uncertain, and our activities have decreased considerably. Otherwise, we have both enjoyed retirement and have seen a good share of the U.S., been to Canada twice, and went on a mission trip to Puerto Rico for our church several years ago. Our main concern is a lack of provision for long-term health care.

— Kurt, age 78, retired at age 65

The worst situation with which we have had to be concerned has been the decline of my mother-in-law's health. Soon she will be 96 and has had to deal with several falls and broken bones during the past three years. As a result, it was necessary for us to move her into a nursing home. As this time, she is adjusting well and improving with every day.

The biggest surprise came during the past three months when I went to the doctor for my annual physical and found that I had developed high blood pressure. The medicine recommended has brought the blood pressure to a safe level, but the changes in lifestyle and work habits have been hard to accept.

—Marlon, age 66, retired at age 65

The first five years of retirement were the best years of my life! We took many trips, remodeled our home, and in general enjoyed our life together. Then my wife was diagnosed with cancer. The next two years were dedicated to licking this problem. After two years of operations, chemotherapy, and radiation treatments, she died three days after our 45th wedding anniversary. Since her death, just getting through each day has been a struggle.

As for advice, I'd suggest retirement at the earliest time possible. Leave when you and your spouse can enjoy each other, unfettered by work, for as long as you can. You never know how long or short the post-retirement happiness will last.

—Jesse, age 66, retired at age 57

My retirement has been depressing due to the loss of my spouse by cancer about the time I retired and a major hemorrhagic (no recovery) stroke two years later. These are the worst experiences of retirement, and the latter the biggest surprise. It has kept me from continuing volunteer work and necessitated a change in residence. The best experience has been my remarriage in 1996. My advice to those considering retirement: Do it now!

—Marty, age 67, retired at age 60

Thank the Lord my wife and I had more than 20 years of retirement together before she passed away.

—Harry, age 88, retired at age 63

I enjoyed my retirement for the freedom about as much as anything else. The only bad time I had was when my wife became sick and died eight years later.

—Selby, age 84, retired at age 65

The Female Slant: PHAD

Ladies, say "fad." Try it out loud, say "fad" again. There are several key transitions that female retirees experience, either shortly before or after their retirement. Only the anatomically-related ones differ from the males.

The terms for women are the same as the terms used earlier in this chapter:

> P = Power
> H = Health
> A = Anxiety
> D = Depression

Power

Women who are retiring from the world of work experience the same transitions that their male counterparts do. The majority of these women have gone through menopause, and those health transitions are history. The obvious shifts in power center around emotional changes due to loss of the supervisory role, loss of socialization, and loss of inside information. Financial losses may occur: lowered retirement income and loss of job perks, such as travel expense accounts, company dining rooms, club dues, and private secretaries. Of all of these, perhaps the greatest loss is being cut off from working associates, only to find that you have few other friends outside those you have known on the job. Feelings of isolation become very real and may be hard to overcome.

Women who work as community volunteers or as the movers and shakers in women's clubs feel the same loss of power when they withdraw from their volunteer posts. Some "retire" due to age, others due to changing times and technology. Often there is a personal rift with other women in the group, which drives the club volunteer away prematurely. More ambitious women struggle with the power transition harder than less ambitious ones. Loss of socialization and loss of inside information are, in fact, losses of power, which are identical for volunteer and working retirees.

Another type of transition is the power challenge that women feel when their spouses retire. Most women have learned to enjoy their freedom as homemakers once the children left; with their spouse's return, they resent taking care of the new "child." At one extreme, the wives put up with their spouse's never-ending questions about *why* things are done a certain way. At the other extreme, their power to manage the household is challenged by the recent intruder. One recently retired professional drove his wife to tell me, "My house, my kitchen, my schedule— he's invaded them!" That's when the hostility transition kicks in. This topic and others related to marriage and partners are developed further in chapter 9.

Health

The "silent passage" is over, on average, around age 55; menopause stops just as retirement planning starts in earnest. Every woman is likely to go through several health transitions either before or after retirement. Some are easy, others are sheer hell.

Skin sags, hair thins and grays, vision blurs. Not much fun, but not killers either. These are cosmetic conditions that can be addressed directly or left alone. A few trips to a good dermatologist, a hair stylist, and an ophthalmologist will bring much relief to those who need to regain some of their youthful look.

Major diseases bring about major health transitions. The breadth of female diseases after menopause is enormous. Several of the most common health concerns of all women around retirement age are discussed briefly, but many other diseases can produce equivalent health transitions.

- Weight gain. My wife calls this creeping obesity. Sometimes coupled with hypothyroidism, weight gain is most likely a result of too much food and too little physical activity. When gravity attacks, normally from the waist down, it is time to strike back at your changing metabolism. The seemingly inevitable increase of two dress sizes does not have to happen.
- Osteoarthritis. Degenerative arthritis of the joints affects women more than men, especially in the knees and hands. Linked to inactivity, this disease strikes half of the population older than 65. Being overweight hastens both the onset as

well as the symptoms, especially in the knees.

- Osteoporosis. Women are much more susceptible than men to develop osteoporosis or "porous bones." Hormone replacement therapy (HRT) will help to inhibit bone loss as well as to reduce the risk of cardiovascular disease. Alternately, certain nonhormonal medicines appear to prevent osteoporosis in post-menopausal women equally well. In either case, inactivity may lead to worsening osteoporosis and to feelings of social isolation. A frank discussion about osteoporosis is a must with your favorite physician. You need not suffer physically or emotionally!

- Incontinence. Cough and dribble; sneeze and dribble. Why me? Stress incontinence, the involuntary loss of urine, develops as muscles around the bladder weaken. It is tough to go back into pads full time, but that is one easy solution. Alternately, your physician or nurse practitioner can help you learn pelvic-floor (Kegel) exercises. But just try to tighten up your perivaginal muscles as you swing a golf club.

- Bladder infections. You used to blame these on too much sex, probably not anymore. These bacterial infections now may be due to occasional incontinence and general cleanliness. These infections are easy to treat; it is the root cause that may be difficult to diagnose.

- Breast lumps. About half of all women have some types of lumps in their breasts. Luckily, the vast majority of lumps is non-cancerous. Any new lump should be examined by a physician immediately. Mammograms are X-ray photos of the breasts, and these pictures can reveal tumors too small to be seen or felt. Every year we rejoice when my wife gets her report, "Your recent mammography exam was normal." If you are over 40, get your screen every year!

- Cancer. Most women regard breast cancer as their most serious health threat. In fact, the leading fatal cancer is lung cancer, but *every* cancer is dangerous. Early detection can lead to successful treatment. The Pap test, developed by Dr. George Papanicolaou as a routine screening procedure, has decreased the death rates from cervical and endometrial cancer. How best to say it: stop smoking, eat fewer calories and less fat, get some exercise, and discuss every possible cancer screen with your physician annually. Trust me! Trust your doctor!

• Heart disease. You have been protected for decades by estrogen, but after menopause your risk increases. Enter HRT to add some estrogen and progestin back into your life. You'll feel better, look great, and live longer. But risk factors still lurk: smoking, blood pressure, cholesterol, stress, obesity, lack of exercise. Have you read the signals? It's time to act.

Now What's Next?

The power is gone (or about to be) and you have experienced some health transitions; you may be a candidate to continue further into PHAD. Chances are good that you'll enter this sequence shortly after retirement. But first, let us see what health concerns women are willing to discuss openly.

WHAT WOMEN ARE WILLING TO DISCUSS ABOUT HEALTH...

My husband's health began to worsen and we didn't get to do all the things we had planned. Go do the things you want to before health factors prevent them.

—Harriet, age 68, retired at age 60

I never dreamed that I would spend so much time in retirement seeking medical care! I'm so thankful to have a spouse who challenges and encourages me to stay active socially, yet understands when I prefer to avoid crowds.

The "golden years" are not all golden, but I'm so grateful to be living in a stimulating community that offers so much to entertain and stimulate the mind and body.

—Laura, age 67, retired at age 60

When you get old, you get farty.

—Louise, age 76, retired at age 62

I had a brain tumor and had to retire early. I enjoyed my job and would not have left so early if not forced to.

—Genevieve, age 73, retired at age 59

I was forced into retirement due to injury—not good—my income was low then and is low now—money to just make ends meet is hard. Day-to-day living is not much to look forward to. Seeing friends is my biggest enjoyment. Keeping in touch is important to me.

—Kora, age 75, retired at age 62

I learned to play billiards after moving to a retirement home. Now at 86, what can the next 10 years bring but failing health and memory?

—Sally, age 86, retired at age 66

I am Maxine's friend and Power of Attorney:

Maxine was happy for the first 10 years after her retirement. She volunteered at her church and the Cancer Foundation, but after 10 years her memory began to fail. She lived alone without any close family. I hired a home companion for her for several years. When her condition became worse, I put her in a nursing home. She now has acute Alzheimer's and is mostly confined to her bed. She doesn't know anyone who visits her. I have sold her home; that money has gone for nursing home expenses. Just recently I sold her farm and that is what is paying her bills now. Her expenses are about $4,000 a month. She has been in a nursing home for 7½ years.

—Maxine, age 85, retired at age 65

My retirement went smoothly and was very satisfying until I had cancer of the breast a year ago. Since then I have lost some sense of security about what had always been my perfect health. For some months my life was a nightmare.

—Marilee, age 70, retired at age 64

Best:

1. Enjoy being with eleven grandchildren and four great grandchildren

2. Children all live within three hours' drive

3. All have happy and successful marriages

Worst:

Health. I am now learning to be mobile with my second hip replacement due to a staph infection. This has left me with vertigo, thus I need a cane to get around.

Advice:

Retire as soon as you are financially capable, i.e., 60 to 65, develop hobbies, keep physically active, make commitments, and volunteer to help others.

—Harlan, age 76, retired at age 66

I miss the association with friends and co-workers. It is quite an adjustment to disassociate yourself from those you enjoyed working with and spent time with for at least 40 hours a week for a long time.

I am surprised that I have adjusted as well as I have. A health problem initiated my retirement, not physically, but needing to spend quality time with my husband.

—Irma, age 63, retired at age 62

My husband retired four years before I retired, and he has had Parkinson's disease. We wanted to travel and enjoy retirement. Retirement has been great. We celebrated our 50th wedding anniversary last year.

—Donna, age 73, retired at age 63

I retired and stayed home to take care of my disabled husband who needed total care after his accident. After much therapy he is better than anyone ever anticipated he could ever be. He's our "Miracle Man"! We do hope in the future to be able to do some fun things that would normally go with retirement.

—Donna, age 64, retired at age 61

I retired to be with my ill husband. We bought a motor home and have traveled through 26 states this summer. We went to Hawaii for two weeks also. I am glad we had our travel dreams come true and will be content to be home in future.

—Mary, age 59, retired at age 58

I was happy to retire as I had an elderly parent to take care of in my home.

—Bonnie, age 67, retired at age 61

My husband died recently. He retired at age 62. I encouraged his early retirement. (I would have liked him to retire at 60). We enjoyed his retirement very much until he became ill with cancer.

The death of a spouse is shattering—beyond anything you anticipate or imagine. Be sure both know all about your finances and planning. You never know which one of you suddenly will have to take over.

—Eunice, age 78, retired at age 60

My husband retired four years before I did because of poor health. Because of his health problems, we were not able to enjoy retirement as we had hoped. My outside activities were limited because my first concern was his welfare. I believe good health is the most important factor in a happy retirement. Without that, nothing else is attainable. While we still enjoyed each other's company and loved each other until his death (52 years of marriage), I cannot say that retirement was fulfilling for us.

—Mildred, age 78, retired at age 67

We were married in 1941, and I was a war bride. We always made good adjustments to life, but illness made retirement more difficult.

My husband should have retired at 65, but other than myself, his interest in life was his profession. However, the year before he retired he was diagnosed with Parkinson's disease. I was his only caregiver for 11 years. We were thankful to do a lot of traveling while he was working. I have lost the desire to travel now that I am alone.

—Rita, age 82, retired at age 67

A = Anxiety, D = Depression

By now your closet door should be ajar, perhaps open wide. Your personal thoughts have surfaced about transitions that might take place when you retire or that have occurred already.

For a few, the transitions are just a breeze, like learning to ride a bike or to line dance. If you sense that your power and health transitions are virtually nonexistent, then you can stop. Men and women alike, you are done now with the retirement sequence. You will have no anxiety, no depression about your retirement. The internal logic: "I am different. None of this applies to me." Maybe...

My survey of retirees suggests that 25% experience anxiety about some aspect of their retirement. Financial worries, separation from work, and health concerns top the list for creating fear and apprehension, both pre- and post-retirement. Luckily, many of these adjustments work out satisfactorily, self-doubt diminishes, and a happy retiree emerges over a period of months to a year or two.

However, another possible outcome related to anxiety is depression. Approximately one retiree in eight (12% to 13%) experiences depression over one or more of the retirement domains. Leading causes are lack of money, separation from work, poor health, and possible relocation. Of course, depression can strike anytime, but often it starts early in retirement.

The medical literature divides anxiety and depression into separate mental states. Diagnostic criteria and symptoms drive psychiatrists into separate and distinct modalities for their treatment. This is discussed at length in the *Diagnostic and Statistical Manual of Mental Disorders (DSM-IV)*, which has been refined over several decades since it was first published in 1952.

That is the problem for the lay writer and the lay reader. I acknowledge the need for very definite criteria to judge a broad spectrum of mental disorders, such as schizophrenia, dissociative, affective, and psychosexual disorders; organic disorders such as Alzheimer's disease; multiple types of personality disorders; and childhood/adolescent disorders, such as hyperactivity and eating disorders.

For purposes of classification in retirement transitions, I generalize that anxiety about retirement is simply a lighter-weight version of depression about retirement. Here is the rationale for this one-dimensional treatment.

First, we will limit the cause to retirement alone, knowing that there are additional factors that may limit our understanding. Second, we see a kind of continuum (sometimes called an "axis") between the criteria for anxiety and depression. Third, our collective experience says this simple approach works: a continuum model is much simpler to understand in our daily lives.

The most common type of anxiety is called generalized anxiety disorder (GAD). This is well characterized by chronic worry and tension. This state of mind anticipates disaster in dimensions such as health, finances, family, and work. Anxious about their retirement, people become unable to relax, unable to concentrate, unable to enjoy life's pleasures, even unable to sleep. Sometimes physical symptoms become very real: headache, irritability, sweating, lightheadedness, nausea, and impotence (ED). Some people experience phobias, irrational but real fears of social situations with their family or co-workers, or darkness and closed-in places, such as elevators, airplanes and tunnels.

Typically, anxiety is based on actual or fantasized experiences from the past or in the future. How easy it is to become anxious about the unknown transitions involved with our retirement.

Let us contrast with the other end of this continuum: depression. The symptoms are not the same for everyone, but if you experience four or five of these acutely for two weeks or more, you may be experiencing depression:

- A persistent sad, anxious or "empty" mood
- Sleeping too little or sleeping too much
- Reduced appetite and weight loss, or increased appetite and weight gain
- Loss of interest or pleasure in activities once enjoyed, including sex
- Restlessness or irritability

- Persistent physical symptoms that do not respond to treatment (such as headaches, chronic pain, or constipation and other digestive disorders)
- Difficulty concentrating, remembering, or making decisions
- Fatigue or loss of energy
- Feeling guilty, hopeless, or worthless
- Thoughts of death or suicide

You can see the extension of anxiety into depression, whether it be mild or major depression. The continuum approach for those about to retire is especially valuable, because it allows you to gauge the extent of your personal transition into anxiety and depression. The principle is simple: **If you feel anxiety over health changes in your life, get help. You may sink into needless depression.**

The way out takes time. First, there is the very personal sharing and communication of your symptoms and problems with your spouse, your partner, or your best friend. Talking about what bothers you—not about Freud, Jung, and your toilet training—really helps. A few sessions with a trained professional in counseling and psychotherapy may be needed. Talk therapy really works whether it is in a bar, in bed, or in a counselor's office.

Your primary physician is the next stop. Your doctor has the diagnostic training as well as an arsenal of psychotherapeutic agents—anti-anxiety and antidepressant medicines. Many of these are very effective, I am sure, but my only experience was disappointing. After a cursory diagnosis, I tried a well-known, non-addictive medicine for anxiety several years ago. It turned me inside out and upside down, emotionally and physically. When I returned to my physician, he told me that he had 20 more medicines we could try. That is when I changed physicians; his shotgun approach was too cavalier for me.

Instead, I tried two other strategies. First, I used the tincture of time in order to more fully grasp what was bothering me. Next, I sought help from a pharmacy professor who told me about St. John's Wort. This is an over-the-counter herbal supplement that has been known for centuries to ease stress and promote feelings of well-being. My pharmacist helped me select a brand that is well-known for its standardization of active ingredients. St. John's Wort worked!

It was during this period that I discovered the generality of the "fad" transitions for almost all retirees. I worked through my own transitions, and after a few months I stopped taking St. John's Wort.

The bottom line: transitions due to power shifts and health changes around the time you retire are inevitable. If you need help to work through your personal transitions, get help first by talk therapy. If this doesn't work, see your medical doctor promptly. *Don't fool around*, hoping your distress will go away by itself. In time, you will learn how to kick-back and enjoy the freedom of your retirement!

My Personal Space: To Your Health

What new activities can you add to improve your physical health? Walking daily with a buddy, pedaling a bike at a health club, something more strenuous—possibly aerobics? Could you lower your Body Mass Index (BMI)?

What can you shed? Twenty pounds, desserts, alcohol?

Can you list your prescription medicines by name, dose, and frequency? Your vital stats: weight, blood pressure (systolic/diastolic), cholesterol (LDL, HDL, and triglycerides), fasting blood sugar (glucose), and Body Mass Index (BMI)?

Forgetful about names? Have you tried any new methods to improve your memory? To challenge your daily routine, to relieve boredom?

Forgetful about your yearly medical check-up? Routine medical screening tests? Self-examination for moles, skin cancer, or breast cancer? You owe it to yourself and to your spouse or partner to get a current medical exam and the necessary tests!

Chapter 8
Love Thy Neighbor

- Volunteering a few hours every week is important to me.
- I volunteer regularly for community service activities.
- I have taken on too many volunteer activities.
- Religious activities are an important part of my life.
- I can't wait to see what the next few years will bring.
- I contribute something to a major charity every year.

Alexis de Tocqueville was the first to describe volunteerism in fledgling America. His book, *Democracy in America*, first published in 1835, ranks volunteerism with liberty, freedom, and equality in both colonial and pioneer life. Helping others was—and continues to be—a hallmark of American democracy.

Two movements have flourished, one at the national level and a second within our states and communities. Within the last two decades, strong national programs have emerged to help organize the country: The Points of Light Foundation, America's Promise—The Alliance for Youth, and the Corporation for National and Community Service. Have you heard of service initiatives such as AmeriCorps, Campus Compact, Learn and Serve America, RSVP, SCORE, or VISTA?

Over one half-million Americans, age 55 and over, serve in Senior Corps programs: RSVP (Retired and Senior Volunteer Program), Senior Companion Program, and Foster Grandparents Program. RSVP volunteers do almost anything—from helping the terminally ill, to teaching recent immigrants English, to conducting environmental surveys. Senior Companions help frail and elderly adults sustain their independence, while Foster Grandparents offer personal support to children with special needs: abused and troubled teens; young mothers; premature infants; and kids with disabilities. Grandparents know how to give, especially to children.

Who hasn't heard of "Make a Difference Day"? Late in October, annually, two million Americans of all ages spend a day helping others. Where? In their local communities and neighborhoods. In the spring, *USA WEEKEND* chronicles outstanding examples and celebrates the remarkable accomplishments of volunteers all across America.

The hallmark first identified by de Tocqueville still gleams!

Community Connections

Despite all this activity, only 40% of retirees report positive feelings about helping others through community service. Some retirees have spent much of their adult lives doing volunteer work, while others are just beginning to find the time. Retirees serve in a myriad of ways: hospitals and human services, homelessness and hunger, youth programs, adult recreation, arts education, and environmental activities.

Whatever approach you adopt, the principle is the same: **Your community needs your help. You can help by volunteering.**

What are your strengths, perhaps your likes and dislikes? Could you proofread brochures, assist in a juvenile court, take kids to the zoo, or help a United Way agency with its accounting, perhaps as an extension of your former work?

My own experience relates to Meals on Wheels, often a noon luncheon program for shut-ins. My mother lived alone 900 miles away and was confined to her home after major surgery. She needed ready-to-eat Meals on Wheels. Beyond the hot lunch and evening snack, the volunteer drivers provided some brief socialization for her daily. Even though her need was temporary, Meals on Wheels was there, no red tape, no delays. I have the greatest thanks and praise for the wonderful volunteers who provided this service. More importantly, now I understand the nature of social service throughout every community.

I am enjoying my retirement. I particularly enjoy freedom to spend my time "my" way. I enjoy my lazy mornings. I keep active. I do volunteer clerical work at a major health facility two to three days a week. I put in four to five hours each day. Retirement is great.

—Bertha, age 70, retired at age 67

I volunteer in the Finance Office at church every Monday, Habitat for Humanity every Thursday morning, and then go to the Thrift Clothes Shop and work until 10 p.m.—a long day. I have held many positions there.

Still do our cooking, laundry, and bookkeeping. Don't have time to get bored or depressed.

Our son gave me a computer for Christmas, and I'm having a ball. I e-mail far away friends and play a few games now and then.

Free advice: Don't leave the area, your church, and friends; seeing friends move away or die is the worst.

—Mary, age 80, retired at age 63

I have enjoyed retirement. I spend two mornings as a Red Coat at the hospital. So far I have 4,500 hours in. I work three days a week as a carpenter on houses for Habitat for Humanity. In my free time I do volunteer work for my church, the Boy Scouts, Thrift Clothes Shop, etc.

Both my wife and I enjoy reasonably good health, so that we can enjoy active travel vacations.

—Dwight, age 83, retired at age 65

My wife and I are busy in the Church Women United Food Pantry in the community. We buy supplies, transport eggs and bread, and fill in as persons distributing food when the people assigned cannot be there.

—Marvin, age 78, retired at age 65

Retirement is wonderful! I remember that my blood pressure soon dropped enough to go off medication. My first year of retirement was spent playing golf and doing gardening, lawn work, etc. The second year I started volunteering at one of the local hospitals (two days of four hours each). I have quit the golf and really enjoy the volunteer work. I meet a lot of people, and I get plenty of walking exercise in doing so.

—Ralph, age 64, retired at age 61

After I retired, I attended a Leadership Academy to acquaint myself with the various agencies needing volunteers. I chose the Urban Ministry, where I served 10 years as a volunteer driving for Meals on Wheels. Currently, I drive once a week.

My advice to new or potential retirees is, "Get involved."

—Kirk, age 73, retired at age 59

As my health and physical well-being have been excellent during post-retirement, I now wish I had asked to continue employment for another five years. During those years I was somewhat lost for activity that gave fulfillment of time and purpose.

I found myself volunteering at the local hospital, and I have a tenure of 2,500 hours to date.

Advice: find an activity to fill the gift of time.

—Jeremy, age 80, retired at age 65

I had looked forward to my 65th birthday as that meant I was at the age of retirement. For several weeks afterward I found that I couldn't seem to do any household chores because I felt that "I had tomorrow to do it." So in order to be helpful to others, I started my volunteer work at the hospital and became more involved in church activities and clubs. Now I find I'm so busy that I often wonder how I found time to be employed. I do miss the wonderful staff and friends I worked with for many years.

—Cynthia, age 76, retired at age 65

I spend most of my time doing volunteer work at my church and social service organizations. I have been a board member for about 13 years and work with the homeless. In fact, I tell people I had more free time for activities (golf) while I was employed than I do now.

—Jerome, age 62, retired at age 57

Finding Fulfillment

Caregivers of all kinds have compassion. Do you? Can you spot distress? Are you sympathetic? Do you have a desire to help? *Do* you help?

Beyond the strictly spiritual, religious institutions present unique opportunities for outreach to members in need as well as to the local community. Helping shut-ins do their shopping, keep medical appointments, and attend religious services are but a few examples. Sometimes congregations focus on issues of food and shelter; other ministries work to improve social justice. Teams of trained volunteers, often college students, build houses, refurbish schools, create drinking water systems, and even dig latrines. In every case, a huge measure of compassion flows outward.

Do you have a family member in need? An aging parent who lives with you and needs care around-the-clock? A child or grandchild who is disabled? A spouse with limited mobility? If you are a principal caregiver, you may not have much time or energy left over for community projects. That is easy to understand, but your own sanity also is important. Limited community outreach may be *your* therapy.

Hospice is becoming a reality across America. Over 2,500 dedicated hospice programs provide care for dying people and offer help to their families at every stage of grief and eventual loss. Volunteers are needed for child and family support programs, bereavement programs, nursing home programs and hospice house programs. In every case, hospice provides exceptional support to those with life-threatening illnesses and to their families. End-of-life issues are a reality for every one of us. However, it takes a special combination of compassion, commitment, and dedication to serve the dying.

Could you learn to serve?

My Personal Space: Love Thy Neighbor

Who are your closest relatives? Close by current association or close only by distance? What are their greatest needs?

Does your spouse need special assistance?

Who are your closest friends? Why are they closest?

What can you do to increase the size and scope of your personal network? Could you strengthen a personal relationship that has faltered?

Can you volunteer a few hours every week at a local food kitchen, church office, hospital, or United Way Agency? Habitat for Humanity? YMCA, YWCA—this list never ends—with a friend or relative?

HELPING OTHERS: WHAT SOME RETIREES SAY...

My wife has several illnesses; she is on oxygen and can't drive. I take her to all her doctor appointments. I took a break to walk one mile with my wife. I carry her oxygen tank so she can walk that far.

—Bob, age 69, retired at age 61

I was often disgusted the first year of my retirement with the large amount of physical work I put into preparing our home of 25 years for sale and doing the same for the house we moved to—painting, eaves, roof, landscaping—was this the deserved lot of retirees? However, the move was made to facilitate the giving of more of our time and care to a disabled grandchild whose development and academic achievement in the meantime have been the best rewards of our retirement.

—John, age 83, retired at age 66

I retired to be a caregiver to a member of my family for several years. I was busy. My biggest surprise was that I did not miss my work, just the people I worked with.

—Norma, age 77, retired at age 63

Retirement to me has been a continuation of my work-life and an appreciation for 10,000 blessings. Advice to others? Keep doing what makes you happy and helpful to others. Put people first; ideas, knowledge, morality second; and material things third. Works great.

—Jacob, age 80, retired at age 70

The best—100% busy with community and church work helping others!

—Claude, age 76, retired at age 65

Enjoy life. Try new activities in the community—volunteer, participate—do not "run your battery down." Select among your commitments and decide favorites. Winnow out those you do not really wish to retain. Quiet, private time is very important in the total aspects of retirement.

—Nora, age 78, retired at age 70

Be a good neighbor, whenever and whatever your circumstances.

—Beulah, age 79, retired at age 65

Invest your time, talents, and treasures in the community and in others. You will find real joy and many rewards.

—Nell, age 74, retired at age 58

Don't sit around, get busy and do something for others! My observation is that those who don't soon are gone.

—Wiley, age 78, retired at age 70

I retired early in my career to pursue a God-given calling into full-time Christian service. I am on staff 40-plus hours per week and love every minute of it.

—Carl, age 52, retired at age 51

It is easy to become involved in too many things! You are retired and think you have the time. However, do get involved in community projects that are interesting and enjoyable to you.

—Mimi, age 75, retired at age 65

Chapter 9

Secrets

- "The best part is having time to spend with grandkids. The worst part is taking orders from my wife."
- "Relationships with spouse: difference in physical capabilities, difference in sexual interest, continual presence of retiree at home."
- "Someone asked me how I liked my husband underfoot—we were at our summer home. I said, 'When I get enough of him, I go to the beach to pick agates—boy, have I got agate!'"
- "I retired, but my other half didn't change to retirement mode. This and the fact we were not as close and communicating well, we sold the farm, split our worldly goods, and divorced. I am now happily remarried."

Retirement brings out a quirky side of marriage. Both spouses are affected, but odds favor that recently retired husbands behave more strangely than their wives. One of our close friends retired at age 50 and has been at home with his wife for over 20 years. At one time he alphabetized her spices; for years he has walked up and down two flights of stairs well over 100 times daily. Simple: he needs the exercise; equally simple: he is driving his wife nuts.

Another one of our good friends shops daily at a local supermarket. My wife asked her why daily, knowing very well that her prior shopping pattern had been weekly. The reply, "I'll do anything to get out of the house. He's driving me crazy." He, of course, is her recently retired husband, now at home, underfoot every day.

When I was actively surveying retirees and studying narratives written by them, I found a wife-husband pair who wrote, independently, the following terse comments about their retirement:

- Wife: "It's a wonderful life!"
- Husband: "Ha! Ha!"

My instincts told me to read further and read carefully; there was an underground—a secret story—to be shared by many retirees.

At about the same time, Ann Landers ran a set of columns that spoke of the trauma which ensues when a husband moves home after many years of working. "Just about Had It in West Virginia" wrote, "Retirement stinks," followed by a blow-by-blow description of her husband's bizarre behavior at home. He had, knowingly or not, challenged his wife's ability (and right) to run the household as she had for many years.

That letter was followed by one from a "Daughter in South Dakota," who suggested that her retired father was looking for a role that will make him feel important again. Her conclusion was that the home manager's job already had been filled—by her mother, years earlier.

Two quick follow-up letters appeared about retiree husbands. These embrace opposing points of view:

- Totally Anonymous: "Now I know why God allows women like me to live longer than men. It's so we can have a little peace before we die."
- Alfred's Wife in Clements, CA: "Do I get tired of having him underfoot? Heavens, no. Life goes on as it did before, and I enjoy his company as much as ever…some of us think it's nice to have a guy around the house."

Turn the clock back for a quick trip down memory lane. Do you recall some of the burning issues in the early years of your own marriage? Table 9.1 offers a refresher course as well as a preview of how these same concerns play out at retirement. Many of the early concerns are history, especially the biological ones. Those that remain are the bedrock values in every good marriage.

After retirement a new set of issues crops up. Not every retiree, not every marriage is impacted with the concerns listed as "New Concerns"

in Table 9.1, but most are. Like all issues in marriage, there is an incu-
bation period, a confrontational activity, and then resolution. If there is
a new aspect to the new issues, it is the combination of age and time.
We finally get to an age when we speak our minds, right or wrong. We
also have plenty of time together, most often at home, to nag, to annoy,
to "help" our spouses do things they have probably done well for 40
years or more.

George is 71 years old and has been retired for five years. His essay
illustrates the tensions that keep marriage alive and well during the early
years of retirement. Here are George's views on some marital transitions
faced by him and his wife:

> My biggest surprise in retirement is to find how frustrating it is
> to my wife to have me around the house a much greater amount
> of time than when actively working. She is a type "A" person
> and I am type "B," which we have known for years, e.g., she
> is the early riser, the morning person, the go-go-go type. I am a
> late night person, basically a very optimistic type, much more
> laid back on routine matters that I consider to be "C's" or lower
> on the action list.
>
> If we were in a two-bedroom apartment, it could be a
> disaster! As it is, we are in a three-bedroom house with a full
> basement and a big lot, all of which spreads us out as we work
> toward learning to live together again! We both enjoy outside
> work and I enjoy cooking, whereas she has come to the point
> in her life where meal planning, preparation, and cooking are
> nowhere near the thrill that they were at one time. We keep two
> cars and are both really quite independent. The focus of her life,
> however, is predominantly on our children, housekeeping, and
> outside yard appearance. My focus is on the children, maintain-
> ing the house and property, a nice yard, a comfortable house, all
> with time for other things like reading books, giving back to the
> community, and traveling.
>
> My wife did have a very significant time commitment
> to her elderly parents for the last 15 or more years, including
> several years into retirement, but they have both passed on now.
> We have good interaction with our children (two families). We

continue to move forward on catching up on improvements and remodeling needs to a 45-year-old house, but not as fast as my spouse would like. We have inherited other property that also takes of our time, primarily mine. It is 30 miles away.

In the winter months, I probably prepare four-to-five out of seven evening meals. We prep lunch largely independently on our own schedule and likes, and always breakfast together and enjoy the evening meal together. But meal planning and scheduling also works best for me if I do much of the shopping, which I also enjoy doing and do. But I believe that my wife feels threatened by this change in roles, and we continue to work at better communication. We search for comfortable ground on which neither is dominating the other or the decisions, and I suspect that this communication process will continue for some years into the future. We're having to redefine "turf" and "territory" as to whose right or domain it is, without really wanting to usurp the other's mainstays or needs. We have every confidence we are going to find it!

Table 9.1 Issues in Marriage

In the Beginning: Concerns	At Retirement: Values
Love	Love
Sex	Sex
Birth Control	
Pregnancy	
Children	Children
Child-rearing	Grandchildren
Education	Education
Religion	Religion
In-laws	
Money	Money
Work	

Leisure	Leisure
Friends	Friends
Communication	Communication
Happiness	Happiness

After Retirement: New Concerns

Freedom and Control

Spouses Underfoot

Commitment and Respect

Death of a Spouse

Freedom and Control

A simple solution for wives who have managed their households for years is to make their retired husbands "vice president in charge of nothing." He gets the fancy title and a bit of self-esteem. Next, put him out the door for a few hours every day; he'll enjoy his new freedom even more.

This scenario also works if the wife has been the major breadwinner and retires "to help" her husband at home.

Ideally, communication, interests, and activities match up well after years of marriage, and time together can be spent doing both chores as well as interesting things together. Trouble comes when expectations are unmet.

Case 1. The retired husband announces that he expects to golf with his buddies every day. This is compounded by poker losses and too much beer in the 19th hole, six days out of seven.

Case 2. The wife of a retiree announces that she expects him to paint the closets, refinish a chest, clean out the basement and garage, sweep the roof, prune the evergreens—the list never ends.

Neither set of expectations is very realistic, because they involve major changes of lifestyle. The principle is clear: **Marriage after retirement needs to build on marriage before retirement. Both partners need time, friends, and projects for themselves as well as mutual time and activities together.**

If he wants to unload the dishwasher, bake a loaf of bread, move the den furniture around, or grocery shop, so be it. Just add green maraschino cherries and sliced water chestnuts to his grocery list; that will end his interest in shopping for several weeks, I predict.

If she decides to clean out your closet, relocate your prescription medicines, or schedule you to attend the Art Museum Guild luncheon with her, go with the flow. Isn't your new togetherness wonderful? It can be, if you will do your share.

A healthy dose of good communication infused into the marriage of retirees will reduce the need for control and will elevate the joys of freedom and togetherness.

> My husband was retiring and going to Florida for the winter, so I didn't feel I had a choice…I had to retire…
> —Pearl, age 71, retired at age 53

> For many the greatest adjustment is having much more time spent with your spouse. It is important to allow the freedom for each other to do their own thing.
> —Dwight, age 60, retired at age 59

> My husband was retired for five years before I retired, so it wasn't a matter of both of us retiring at the same time and suddenly being together for 24 hours a day. Be sure to let each other have some breathing room.
> —Emily, age 63, retired at age 60

> I was looking forward to retirement, and I was not disappointed. My husband and I have so much more freedom without schedules. He is nice to have around the house with time out for his special interests. We have been married 52 years. My only advice is to retire at 65 or earlier. Human bodies tend to start wearing

out, and they might miss a lot.

—Elizabeth, age 72, retired at age 59

The best thing about retirement is that I am in total control of my time—I can do what I want to do when I want to do it (within reason, of course—I'm married!).

The biggest surprise was how well my wife and I adapted to retirement, and how much we have been able to do together since retiring.

The best advice to those considering retirement is: Go the first day you are eligible.

—Dave, age 66, retired at age 52

We need a duplex—his side and my side. He retired early and stays at home. My only solution is to keep working. I may never be able to retire!

—Betty, age 68, *not yet retired*

My husband retired two years prior to my retirement. I believe it was helpful for us to retire at separate times so that we did not depend on each other to plan things to do together all the time. We do maintain the same schedule for arising and retiring as we did while we were working.

I have the following suggestions for those contemplating retirement:

1) Make sure your retirement income is approximately the same as your working income.

2) Develop some hobbies and interests outside of work before you retire.

3) Be open to change; maintain an optimistic outlook.

4) Develop a loose structure for your days after you retire.

—Meredith, age 64, retired at age 62

Husbands Underfoot

If he's bored, get him moving; if he sleeps in front of the TV, get him moving. Remember, you are president and he is vice president in charge of nothing. Your trump are higher than his, but you'll have to play them carefully. Perhaps he needs a challenge (not a chore) or a buddy (not a chick). Perhaps you need to ask a friend to call him and plan an afternoon out. Perhaps you *two* need an afternoon or evening out together. Every couple that has worked through 20, 30, or 40 years of marriage surely knows what communication pattern works best—and what doesn't work at all.

The possibilities are endless: Tell a true family story to your grandkids, work on the lawn and shrubs at the library, help with a community festival. Perhaps cleaning the hall closet *together* at an agreed-upon time would have a positive impact on both of you.

> My husband and I have worked out a compatible schedule so that we know where each other is but we don't interact all day. Thus, we have avoided the friction of excessive togetherness. My husband, who has always spent a great deal of time in solitary reading and writing, continues to do that in his at-home study while I work in my study on the top floor. We meet in the kitchen/family room most days for lunch and then about 4:30 to begin unwinding and sharing our day's experiences. Having different biorhythms, we exercise at different times and in different ways. This routine is not necessarily ideal for all couples, but it has worked for us.
>
> —Lila, age 65, retired at age 62

> The best thing about retirement is being able to do what you want to when you want to. The worst part is gloomy days. My biggest surprise is how well my wife and I adjusted to being together so much.
>
> —Ryan, age 72, retired at age 58

> My spouse retired at an earlier age than I had expected. His many interests, crammed into evenings and weekends when working, could now be pursued at a more pleasurable pace, and new ones have been added. He has been content in retirement, and it is great that he is around home so much.
>
> —Melinda, age 67, retired at age 60

Commitment and Respect

The children are married, the grandkids are in high school, and you have been married for 40 years. Have you made many adjustments along the way? Zillions!

Even if your marriage vows are stronger now than ever, hang on tight: there are more changes coming. These should be easy for both of you because they involve mutual love—both physical and mental.

Your marriage should be entering a stage where mutual commitment and respect reign supreme. You know what each other likes doing and dislikes doing. You accommodate your daily patterns—your requests and your suggestions—around your partner's needs and wishes. You also know which emotions run highest and lowest with your partner. You adjust your daily patterns to support each other emotionally, rather than to annoy or pick away at the unimportant.

Perhaps a bit of free space is needed by one or both of you daily. You both have some short-term personal projects to accomplish, and these are best done alone. You have poker or bowling on Tuesday nights; she has luncheon bridge on Thursdays. Wonderful! No need to hassle about Tuesday or Thursday meals. Bring Chinese in, eat out, make soup and salad, and stay home.

If you have a mutual goal to paint the spare bedrooms, that's wonderful, too. Paint together, even if one of you is the better painter. There are complementary roles for every wife-husband team.

As ever, an extra measure of good communication is needed to achieve both personal and family goals. The principal issue normally centers on timing, rather than the goals themselves. Your early retirement years are as close to the golden years of marriage as you're likely to get. Enjoy now, while you have your health and each other's company.

> The spouse of a retired individual often has the most difficult adjustments to make. Fortunately, in my case my spouse had been employed all during our marriage, and she also prepared for her own retirement, which she took early in order that we could both enjoy a similar situation rather than one working and the other not.
>
> It is very important that a retired person be engaged in an

activity that in some ways parallels the pre-retirement demands on that person's time. In my case (and also my spouse), I had become closely involved in several national professional organizations at the executive level; this enabled both of us to continue to stay in the loop of our professions and enjoy the fellowship of our colleagues, both younger and older than we.

Our former and present professional activities required us to do considerable traveling, and also provided us with additional income, which allows us to also engage in personal selective travel that we enjoy so much. Also, we both continue to be very active in environmental and community projects that are very satisfying as well as providing an opportunity to maintain social and professional contacts in the community.

Good health is the greatest asset for a happy retirement. This is not always something of choice, but one can work toward that end by engaging in healthful activities all through one's life.

—Boyd, age 81, retired at age 65

If married, both you and your spouse must be ready for retirement and committed to make it successful. Travel has been our secret to success.

—Hank, age 63, retired at age 60

Time to give more attention to my wife and to help her so she can be a little bit "retired" too!! It has been fun! We enjoy each other's company. No major or life threatening illnesses for my wife or myself has allowed us to enjoy retirement to the fullest. We are thankful for our good health. My motto: I was born to retire!! It has been a most positive time in my life.

—Leland, age 73, retired at age 65

My wife and I are in reasonably good health and enjoying each other with the wisdom of age and an appreciation for the preciousness of time.

—Dale, age 82, retired at age 66

My life continues much the same as it did before retirement as my husband continues to work in his profession. We do, however, enjoy the freedom of setting our own hours and vacation times. The pressure is much less. We also never lack for something to do.

—Janet, age 72, retired at age 63

My Personal Space: Secrets

Secrets are out, communication is in, especially so within marriage. Can you list one or two recent examples where you and your spouse or partner have misconnected? Where an extra measure of communication would have defused an issue before it happened?

What bugs you most about your retirement? What bugs your spouse most about your retirement? About their retirement? Could you talk this one over today—just the two of you—with an open, positive, proactive approach?

What's left to be silent about? To brood over? Money, family, and sex come to mind easily, of course. Why worry needlessly when a few minutes of give-and-take with the right person will bring joy to your heart and, quite possibly, to theirs, too?

Death of a Spouse

Can you imagine the isolation, frustration, and loneliness that set in after the death of a spouse? Probably not at this time. Be assured: When death comes, when the funeral is over, when the estate is settled, lonely isolation will creep in. This is the time to take inventory of your own life.

What have you missed in life so far? *Do it.* What immediate goals to set? *Set one or two.* What careful moves to make? *Be prudent.* You are alive with much to offer; the major questions are what, how, and with whom? You will survive better if you reestablish some of your social contacts with family and friends first, then see what develops in time.

If death of your spouse occurs shortly before retirement or soon thereafter, you will feel cheated, and properly so. You have spent much of your married life working and now are robbed of some of the most joyful years together. Whatever your age, you might have 20 or more years left. Plan now for this eventuality; *you* might be the surviving spouse!

As a post-script to this brief commentary on death, you might wonder how those who never married feel about their retirement. Two opposing views are included in the retirees' comments for balance.

Conclusions: 1) life is for the living; 2) good health and happiness are goals worth pursuing; and 3) decisions have consequences. Sir Francis Bacon reflected upon when a man should marry: "A young man not yet, an elder man not at all." I do not agree with that advice; do you?

> The best of retirement was that I was able to take care of my wife, who became ill with cancer. I was able to be with her day and night.
>
> The worst was her passing away before we got to do all we intended to do. We did travel some, but she had to stop when she became too ill.
>
> Biggest surprise was how much work my wife did while I was working. Since I have retired, I am busy most of the time. I have had to be the bookkeeper, dishwasher, house cleaner, go here, go there…I keep very busy.
>
> —Rex, age 70, retired at age 61

> Wills make material arrangements, but sense of loss and deprivation at death of a spouse are worrisome for the surviving partner.
>
> —Blake, age 78, retired at age 66

> The worst of my retirement was the death of my husband while we were in Minnesota on vacation. We were retired just one year.
>
> —Loretta, age 79, retired at age 62

> I remarried after losing my wife to cancer just prior to retirement. I am now happily married again after five years.
>
> —Jim, age 66, retired at age 59

> The only positive aspect of my retirement has been the opportunity it provided for younger faculty members! My work was the center of my life. I loved teaching, writing, speaking on the

national level, every facet of my work. I never married, which I think narrowed my "life view" considerably. I miss the involvement with students and older faculty members. I'm very busy (writing a textbook, for example), but my life is much less fulfilling than it was during my thirty-plus years of employment.

—Susan, age 70, retired at age 66

I retired at 55—it was wanted and carefully planned. As a single person I do miss much of the interaction with colleagues at work—that has been the only disadvantage for me. I would not have retired early except that I have my own business and am heavily involved in volunteer work for a professional organization—and this keeps me even busier than I had expected.

I am happy in retirement and especially enjoy being able to make my own work schedule.

—Martha, age 67, retired at age 55

Chapter 10

What Really Matters?

I am your master,
I can make you rise or fall,
I can work for you or against you.
I can make you a success or a failure.
I control the way you feel and the way you act.
I can make you laugh, work, and love.
I can make your heart sing with joy, excitement, and elation, or
I can make you wretched, dejected, or morbid.
I am your *attitude*!

—Anonymous

Similar age. Similar retirement income. Similar health. Similar family circumstances. One retiree appears to be very happy with retirement while another is unhappy, feeling negative, if not depressed. Why?

The first principle in chapter 2 indicates that all domains correlate positively with happiness in retirement. For purposes of discussion, we equate and interchange some terms in order to broaden the concept of happiness; we will use happiness, satisfaction, fulfillment, and success interchangeably, knowing that there are subtle differences in their meanings.

How satisfied will you be as a retiree? How happy? Your domain scores are one measure; you should have charted them in chapter 2. If your scores fall in the High Range, you should be happy, fulfilled, and successful in your retirement.

Chances are good that you have one or more domain scores in the

Low Range. If so, that is your clue that some thoughtful effort will be needed to find inner peace when you retire.

With these possibilities in mind, perhaps you would like to compare your domain scores with those given in Table 10.1. The domains are rank-ordered in importance to retirees; the scores for each domain represent average (mean) values of 700 retirees.

Table 10.1 Domain Scores

Domain	Low Scores Below	Average Range	High Scores Above
Freedom and Leisure (F&L)	34	34 to 45	45
Finances (F)	16	16 to 25	25
Work (W)	19	19 to 25	25
Family and Friends (F&F)	13	13 to 17	17
Health (H)	17	17 to 22	22
Helping Others (HO)	9	9 to 15	15

For example, the Freedom and Leisure (F&L) domain score for all retirees is 40 and the standard deviation (SD) is approximately 5.5. Two-thirds of all F&L domain scores fall in the Average Range between 34 and 45, that is, 40 plus or minus one SD. The remaining one-third of the scores is split between the High Range and the Low Range.

Now you can assess your own domain scores more critically. Do your scores fall into the average range? Are any in the high or low ranges? If so, you fall into the uppermost or lowermost 16% of the retiree population in those domains.

The principle that will help you predict your success in retirement is as follows: **The higher your domain scores, the happier you will be. Retirees who score in the high range across all the domains will be the most fulfilled.**

A Higher Magnification

In this section, we examine those retirees who scored above average in *any* of the six domains. These results are given in Table 10.2.

The column of "Percent Highest Scorers" shows that 29% of the retirees scored high in at least one domain, 12% scored high in two domains, 5% in three, and 3% in four domains.

Remarkable!

Which domains? It doesn't matter! Happy retirees score uniformly high across any and all of the domains.

Table 10.2 Highest and Lowest Scorers

Number of Domains	Percent Highest Scorers	Percent Lowest Scorers
1	29	31
2	12	19
3	5	7
4	3	2
5	0	1
6	0	0.4

Next we examine the lowest scorers—those retirees who scored below average in *any* of the six domains. The column "Percent Lowest Scorers" shows that 31% of the retirees scored low in one domain, 19% in two domains, 7% in three, and 2% in four. Approximately 10% of the retirees score low in three or more domains. This is the unhappy group that's "flunking" retirement.

Which domains? Those who scored low in one or two domains uniformly report that "helping others" is the weakest aspect of their retirement. In all other cases, retirees score uniformly low across any and all of the domains.

This finding also is remarkable—that one activity, helping others, is lacking in the lives of half of the retirees.

You should compare the number of your own highest and lowest scores with the above analysis. Will you be a happy retiree? Or will you flunk retirement?

Life Events

In addition to the survey instrument, many retirees wrote a separate, anonymous narrative about their lives, often with a spin on retirement. This collection of personal vignettes holds answers to the question at hand: What really matters?

The flood of life's stories was divided into the same two groups we dealt with in the prior section. One group of narratives was written by those with the highest domain scores; the other group was written by those with the lowest scores.

These are the same two groups we characterize as "happy" (highest scorers) and "unhappy" (lowest). The two groups were analyzed by gender first.

Are men happier than women? Women happier than men?

The percentages of men and women were the same in the happy group (54% men/46% women) as in the unhappy group (54% men/46% women). No news here.

The same two groups were analyzed for age. The happy group averaged age 70, while the unhappy group was 72. Practically the same age.

The range of life events described in poignant detail is enormous: colon cancer, around-the-clock care of a parent, investments turned sour, divorce of a child, death of a grandchild, major surgery, death of a spouse, entry into a nursing home—there is no end to the ways retirees have been stressed. These same life events happen to both happy and unhappy retirees. If you live to retirement age and beyond, there is no way to avoid them!

Thus we have the first key to the difference between happy retirees and unhappy retirees. Is it their gender? No! Is it their age? No! Have the happy retirees been subjected to fewer life events and thus to less stress and anxiety? No!

The First Key: Attitude

The first key to a successful retirement is a positive attitude toward life. Retirees who perceive themselves in control of their lives have the ability to cope with all of life's situations. A happy retirement is well-rooted in many years of work, family life, and community participation before retirement. A positive attitude encourages us to remain purposeful, deeply connected to family and friends, open to continued learning from life, and contented with ourselves as human beings.

I am indebted to an anonymous retiree who sent me the following story:

> A farmer who was standing in town was approached by a man who said he was considering moving into town and would like to know how the people were. The farmer said, "What are the people like where you are coming from?" The man replied, "Not very nice people." The farmer said, "That's about the same as the people will be here."
>
> Another man later approached him with the same question and the farmer again replied, "What are the people like where you are coming from?" The man said, "Oh, they are just wonderful people." The farmer said, "That's just about the kind of people you will find here."

The anonymous retiree's conclusion: "If people have enjoyed life, they will enjoy retirement. If they were grumblers, they will continue to grumble about retirement."

> I maintain fairly good health. When I do have problems, I don't dwell on these or talk about them. I am in many activities—some continued from those enjoyed during my teaching years, some added. I volunteer for a variety of activities: church, music, entertainment, gardening, and cooking.
>
> The worst thing in my life is the loss of loved ones— relatives and friends.
>
> The best is the deepening of my faith; always being occupied—spirit, mind, body—seeking new friends and experiences; finding ways to help others. These are important to me because I have no family.
>
> I have been helped by my deep faith:
> • by believing in the good and seeking it,
> • by loving and not hating,
> • by serving rather than being served,

• and by living in the future and not in the past.
—Michelle, age 91, retired at age 65

I consider the best thing about my retirement is that I am master of my time. Of course, health and money are factors to consider. I am limited in activities because of diabetes, but I have a happy outlook on life and I enjoy each day.
—Martha, age 78, retired at age 62

The best part of retirement is how much fun it can be—the freedom to choose activities to do and not to do, the opportunity to be in the sun and fresh air in the middle of the afternoon, the ability to do something for a friend at the time that is convenient or necessary for the friend, a Saturday afternoon that is open to use in some spontaneous way.

If both members of the couple have been actively engaged in separate professional activities, the biggest surprise can be how many decisions need to be discussed and negotiated each day if they are to do more together again. This requires considerable patience and a spirit of teamwork.

The most critical elements in a successful retirement are similar to what is required in a successful career—curiosity, a positive attitude, and being with people who have a positive attitude.
—Marilyn, age 68, retired at age 65

Advice: Keep a positive attitude, maintain a sense of humor, keep busy. Make friends, enjoy people, enjoy every day by finding something good and interesting to do.
—Hugh, age 95, retired at age 69

One could always use more money; the secret is to be content with what you have.
—Miles, age 61, retired at age 56

After a few weeks of adjustment in "un-peeling" my sense of responsibility, my retirement has been extremely enjoyable and satisfying for both my spouse and myself. The sense of freedom to do what one likes when one likes is refreshing. My wife and I are very fortunate in that we enjoy each others' company and our ability to travel. Raising six successful children makes our years at home worth it. We have been blessed.

—Cliff, age 71, retired at age 62

I certainly was not excited about retirement. I picked up a very enjoyable part-time job, then took on some community projects. Suggestion: Make your work fun, take your fun seriously, and retire with the mixture in mind.

—Frank, age 57, retired at age 52

Live modestly and save diligently so you have resources with which to enjoy retirement. Many of the best experiences in life— a walk in the woods, singing around a piano, watching a sunset, sniffing a daffodil—cost little or nothing.

—Sam, age 68, retired at age 67

I was eating lunch shortly after retirement and a lovely young waitress flirted with me the entire time. As I was leaving with my male ego in top form, she made a point of coming over to say something. "I've been watching you all through the lunch hour and I just had to tell you…you look just like my grandfather!" Poof!

—Lou, age 59, retired at age 55

I found that income after retirement does not keep you in the same lifestyle due to the rise of cost of living. Also, insurance becomes a major problem. Unless one plans very hard for many years before retirement, it is tough, as one must drop their level of living. However, my income as it was during my years of employment and the cost of living, combined, left very little to put away for retirement, and the pension for some wage levels is not enough. I think that employers as well as Social Security think that once you become older, you should just hang it up and stop living. Do I sound bitter? Well, I am.

—Mary, age 68, retired at age 66

My retirement income falls far short of what I ever would have expected and has given me a sense of insecurity and unhappiness about my future.

—Julia, age 71, retired at age 62

After 38 years of public service, I decided to join my son in the aviation business. That business continues, with several other duties that occupy four days each week.

The down part of retirement has been diagnosis of leukemia six years ago and melanoma cancer last year. I am managing both illnesses well and maintain a busy life. My advice to new retirees is keep busy with work, projects, at least one sport, and many social activities.

—Terrence, age 72, retired at age 61

I believe that the key to enjoying retirement is to stay active, keeping your body and mind in as good of shape as possible. My spouse and I walk three miles five days a week, and I enjoy playing golf about three days a week. We enjoy convocations, the local symphony, and attend lectures that we both think we will enjoy.

—Bill, age 75, retired at age 68

The Second Key: Coping

Coping is the second key to a successful retirement. How we deal with life's challenges is likely to affect their eventual outcomes—positive or negative. Handling events realistically and flexibly normally produces more positive results than employing defense mechanisms, such as repression or denial.

A few simple examples of coping strategies follow:

- Playing the hand you are dealt.
- Keeping busy, especially with family and friends.

- Getting help, support, and advice when you need it.
- Solving problems within your physical and emotional resources.
- Realizing that there are no perfect solutions, just better or worse alternatives.
- Grieving, reflecting, and then moving on.

We use these and many other strategies in our daily lives, depending on our personality and the specific demands placed upon us.

At first my husband hadn't retired as yet (my purpose for retiring was to get him to retire). We wanted to spend time together. He worked nights for many years, and I worked days (not easy to adjust). I retired. We had to learn to be together again.
—Rosalind, age 65, retired at age 63

I discovered that my wife was not prepared for my being in her "domain." It has worked well that she went back to work several days each week.
—Frank, age 64, retired at age 63

Retirement has been great. My time is filled with family activities and hobbies. I've taken up new hobbies, such as woodworking, along with my current hobbies of hunting, fishing, golf, and traveling. My wife and I have purchased several get-away cottages— one by a lake and one in a wooded, rural location.

I think the secret to my happiness is broad interests and social activities. I haven't focused on one activity or hobby, but many. Experimenting with activities, such as watercolor painting and down-hill skiing, has kept life challenging and fun.
—Rodney, age 58, retired at age 53

My wife and I had 15 wonderful years of retirement. Our early planning for retirement enabled us to do a lot of traveling. This plus our hobbies kept us busy and happy. However, we were unprepared for my wife's development of Alzheimer's, which necessitated her being in a nursing home for two years. Our health insurance did not cover such a long-term illness; however, we were able to cover all expenses.

I would like to suggest the following for future retirees: 1) start planning early for retirement; 2) keep busy with hobbies, part-time employment, volunteering; 3) prepare for the unexpected.

—Glen, age 88, retired at age 65

The company doctor was pushing for return to work after surgery, and I wasn't able. So I retired early and recuperated leisurely. The job I was doing was heavy and was filled by two men after I left.

—Della, age 67, retired at age 51

I retired early to care for a terminally ill wife and an aged mother. The first two and a half years were not good due to constant need for my attention and care. Since their deaths, I have been free to do what I want, travel when I want, and stay home to do what I want with philately, reading, TV, computers, and other interests. The worst things I have had to deal with were my wife's and mother's deaths, and, recently, the loss of one of my five children. I sometimes feel lonely, but three of my children and grandchildren are close and help me to overcome that feeling.

I would strongly recommend to anyone contemplating retirement that if they are financially sound, do it!

—Marsh, age 65, retired at age 58

Retirement is great! I worked part-time and did volunteer work for the first five years. But my plans and life were changed for me. I now live with, and am caregiver for, my 94-year-old mother who has terminal cancer. I do plan on going back to part-time work later on, God willing. My advice: remember all your plans can be changed by circumstances you can't control. Be prepared to be flexible.

—Tillie, age 69, retired at age 62

When my husband of 59 years died two years ago, I sold both houses and moved to a retirement village. Although the unfillable void remained, life here is very pleasant amongst old and new friends. Our children and grandchildren, all out of state, visit often and keep in touch. I manage to travel to all their special occasions, graduations, marriages, award presentations, etc.

Here I have leisure to live at a comfortable, slowed pace, not only free from responsibilities of homemaking, but free to pursue my longtime reading and studying interests in depth. There are always opportunities to be useful and to contribute to the community. It is a joy to keep up correspondence with friends and former students all over the world. Life is good!

—Helen, age 82, retired at age 68

My wife of approximately 50 years died of cancer. After a year and a half, I remarried. She is an old acquaintance. We have been very happy, enjoying each other's company, traveling, meeting each other's friends, planning new adventures, setting priorities about family gatherings, and in general, looking ahead to our lives together—not looking back on the past.

—Jim, age 75, retired at age 62

My retirement has been one of the best stages in my life. It has given me time to further my education, travel, spend more time on hobbies and other activities, and provide caregiving assistance. However, I lost my spouse to cancer after only one year into my retirement. As a result, I have been pursuing more family involvement, volunteerism, travel, and even part-time employment.

I believe that retirement must be planned early in employment to be successful—both financially and psychologically. It is a wonderful time in life.

—Vera, age 63, retired at age 62

My story and advice are directed to single women. The best happens immediately: no alarm clocks, eat only when hungry, stay up late at night, do household chores throughout week instead of only on weekends, dress for comfort.

The worst creeps in gradually: loneliness, missing co-workers, not being needed or a part of anything.

Advice: Have substantial savings for emergencies; use any IRA funds at a minimum amount; own residence so expenses will be fixed as much as possible. Plan ahead for part-time or temporary employment to feel needed; if alone, consider a pet for companionship.

Retirement has good and bad points. It will happen to everyone at some time. It is not all that great when living alone.

—Katey, age 70, retired at age 63

The Third Key: Helping Others

Making a difference in the lives of others is the third key to a successful retirement. The range of activities that happy retirees report is large: volunteering their service to community organizations, helping religious institutions, caring for a family member or neighbor, sharing their time with an underprivileged child, giving their talent and treasure to a good cause, and many more.

Yet half of all retirees report low scores in the Helping Others domain. If you are not already involved, this simple act—helping others—could make your retirement more interesting as well as more fulfilling. If your domain score for Helping Others is low, you should review chapter 8 in detail.

Attitude, coping, and helping others, together, are three keys to finding inner peace during retirement. When events are viewed positively, retirees know that they have influence and control over their lives. Their positive feelings help them to deal positively with others and to know that their own retirement will be purposeful, meaningful, and fulfilling.

My Personal Space: What Really Matters?

What's missing in my life? What to do about it?

How can I give? Forget about money for now. How can I give my talent and my time to help someone or some organization in need?

List two ways that you currently help others—spouse, family, friends,

community organizations. Could you do more? Could you help to orga-
nize a Living-Well-after-50 day? A community Bike-to-Work day? Coun-
try line dancing?

What do my best friends do for others? Could I help them extend
their efforts? Could they help with my volunteer work? Have you asked
them?

WHAT SOME RETIREES SAY...

The worst thing to do before retirement is to get over-anxious
too early. My husband was counting the days for many months
before he retired, and this seemed to make the time go slower. I
learned from his mistake and tried not to get too anxious about
retiring until the last month.

—Carla, age 67, retired at age 62

Retirement is a time of appreciation, not achievement. The many
benefits I'm enjoying are a result of a retirement filled with satisfaction and happiness. Good health has always been a plan for
me, and this contributes to the overall picture.

—Hester, age 83, retired at age 65

The best, freedom to travel, no schedules! The worst, the de-
mise of family and friends, or their health, at a rapid rate. The
retirement environment of family and friends seems to change
rapidly; due to declines in health there is a lack of buddies who
can share activities.

Even though there are many who share in the experience
of being alone due to death of a spouse, it seems nothing can fill
in the onset of loneliness that ensues. A list of needed activities
at time of death of a spouse would be very helpful. What needs
to be done—where, when, and how? How to avoid learning these
things by trial and error?

—Laura, age 79, retired at age 66

I love retirement! Looked forward to it and could not wait! Being single, with no degree, my income was limited—I worked

since I was in high school—I did plan—I did the best I could with a limited income. My expenses are met so far, but I'm on a very limited budget—no travel! I'm always busy—not enough hours in the day...

Most important and enjoyable: volunteering at my church. I love it! Advice: volunteering gives the most satisfaction!

—Dorothy, age 70, retired at age 65

I am the spouse of a retiree and a housewife. I have not really retired. My days are filled with the same activities as always; we do eat out more often.

—Sara, age 70, *not yet retired*

My 1973 retirement was with my first husband, who died in 1977. I married my second husband in 1985. He had retired in 1976 and died in 1997. The best of both retirements was travel. The worst of both retirements was dealing with death, cleaning out houses, and accepting being alone.

—Sarah, age 80, retired at age 55

Retirement is great. It allows me to schedule my day as I desire, within certain bounds, of course. But getting used to it took some time. After working for many years, it was different not being expected to be at work at a certain time each day. It took me about six months to really relax and feel free and to realize that if I didn't get everything done each day, it was okay because I could just do it the next day.

The worst thing about retirement has been the need to admit my husband to a nursing home and what that did to our income and to my morale. It has been really rough.

To those considering retirement, pay careful attention to what working another year or so could do to your retirement benefits, unless immediate health concerns are an issue.

The greatest thing about my retirement is that I can visit the nursing home every day without having to consider a work schedule. Next best is that I can see my children and grandchildren whenever it fits my schedule. I don't have to wait for vacation time.

—Bonnie, age 70, retired at age 64

I could exist on my retirement, but I cannot live on it. I have to work part-time to do what I want to do.

—Reynold, age 60, retired at age 55

I feel that the approach one takes during the first year of retirement is the key to how retirement and the retiree get along. I tried to not change my schedule. That is, I was up early and busy right away. Amazing how fast the day goes when you're busy.

The best part of retirement is that you really don't retire but just do different things—and in my case, things that I really enjoy doing. We bought an older house, and we renovate one room every year or two. This could take forever, but it's very satisfying. Also, I love golf, computers, and woodworking, and have been very fortunate in that I have a part-time job which allows me to do all these things. As expected, the pay isn't good, but working at the golf course in the mornings allows me to meet many new people, many of whom have become very good friends, and doing all their computer programming has been very satisfying. Also, it allows me to play golf every day if I choose. In the afternoons, I make picture frames for one of the frame shops in town. Here again the number of people I meet is great, and it is very satisfying to see a finished picture with my framework around it.

—Rob, age 55, retired at age 51

I got another job after I retired to make ends meet. When I turn 62, I will retire again.

—Jeff, age 60, retired at age 55

Free advice:

1. Pay off the mortgage on your home before retiring. Avoid debt.

2. Recognize energy loss as you age and keep activities within energy limits.

3. Keep in frequent touch with good friends. Find new friends. Avoid people with a negative attitude. Have fun!

4. Review your dress habits. You don't have to wear ties and jackets every day.

—Avery, age 72, retired at age 60

Retirement has freed me to come to a point where I can give myself permission to just be: to realize that I don't have to be doing something every moment of the day, or I don't have to eat everything on my plate; to realize it takes time to learn the value of prayer and quiet solitude, and that it takes even more time to learn to do it.

There were two major revelations that came to me early in retirement. One of these, which took about three weeks, was the realization that I had been born for this assignment. It just felt good—it was a fit. The other, which took about two weeks longer, was that, while I was retired, my spouse was not. I guess that falls in the category of surprise. (Typical male reaction!) Once that was brought gently to my attention we began to really enjoy the specialness of this broader relationship, and were able to give one another the space each of us needed to grow as individuals in the retirement setting, the better to enjoy one another.

The very worst part of retirement has been the loss of my spouse after just seven years in this new phase of life together. Adjusting to the loss of a loved one is never easy, but that's part of life and has to be dealt with.

As with most of life, attitude is critical.

—Buford, age 81, retired at age 65

Chapter 11
Six Important Questions

This book concludes with six important questions, each based on one of the retirement domains. By now you have read many representative answers based on the experience of hundreds of retirees. These may help you create your own answers.

If some of your individual domain scores are high, you will adjust easily to those areas of retirement. Your answers should flow easily. If any of your domain scores are low, your answers to the corresponding questions should be crafted carefully. Those answers are critical to your future happiness.

Now it is your turn. Write down your own personal answers to the six questions below. And when you are finished, you should discuss your future plans with your spouse, your significant other, your children, and your friends. What comments or questions do they have?

> *1. Freedom and Leisure.* How shall I invest my time meaningfully? What is most important about my new freedom of choice?
>
> *2. Finances.* Will my retirement income cover my retirement expenses? Can I afford to stop working? At what age?
>
> *3. Work.* Can I retire from my job abruptly? Do I have a choice? Could I use a transition, such as part-time work? Will I need to find a new job after I retire the first time?
>
> *4. Family and Friends.* Should I relocate to a new community? New city? New state? Rent or buy? Why?
>
> *5. Health.* How can I improve my health after retirement? My physical well-being? My mental outlook, my optimism, my attitude?

6. *Helping Others.* How shall I serve? What age groups interest me? What organizations? Who could use my talents best?

All during your working years there were times when you faced life's transitions at the same time you were holding down a responsible position, one on which you and your significant others depended.

Now you face another transition: the years after work. The good news is that, after you retire, you will have the luxury of working through the transition with more time to handle its varied challenges.

In addition, you are experienced in life. You are wiser, more savvy than ever before. You have a network of people you can turn to for advice, or you can follow your own star.

Finally, finally, it is your turn, your life. Enjoy your retirement!

Appendix A

Retirement: A Work in Progress

I hope you found the Grace Retirement Inventory (GRI) thought-provoking and helpful. Your scores on the six domains are your keys to happiness as a retiree. Your attitudes and your feelings thus will reward you or thwart you in your quest for a successful retirement.

The GRI was first published in 2002. The normal scores (norms) were developed from approximately 700 retirees—a very broad range of male and female retirees representing many occupations, ages, and household incomes. This population and their norms are described in detail in Appendix B.

GRI normative scores may change slowly over the next decade or two; it is possible that the Boomers will have very different attitudes and feelings about their retirement.

You could assist in this ongoing research program by reporting your GRI scores and a minimal amount of demographic information. All such information will be collected anonymously and used for research analysis and future publication of new research findings.

Here's how to help: Copy the table on the following page, complete the entries, and mail it directly to me. Alternately, you could send the same information by e-mail.

I can be reached by e-mail at regrace@purdue.edu or as follows:

Dr. Richard E. Grace
Purdue University
MSE/ARMS 2219
701 West Stadium Avenue
West Lafayette, IN 47907-2045

GRI Scores and Demographics

	Your Score
Freedom and Leisure (F&L)	_____
Finances (F)	_____
Work (W)	_____
Family and Friends (F&F)	_____
Health (H)	_____
Helping Others (HO)	_____

Demographics

Please enter current date here: _____

Gender: M   F (circle one)   Retired: Yes   No (circle one)

Current age: _____

What year will you (or did you) retire? _____

How old will you be (or were you)

     when you retire(d)? _____

Occupation (Optional) _____

Short comment about retirement (Optional: the best, the worst, the biggest surprise, free advice) _____

_____

_____

_____

_____

_____

_____

_____

_____

_____

Thank you very much for your help!

Appendix B

A Brief Discussion

Most of us like to identify ourselves within large populations. For example, we might want to compare our own age, gender, and household income against what others report. These are summarized in Table B-1 for the two retiree populations that participated in the original survey.

Manufacturing retirees are over 10 years younger, on average, than academic and professional retirees. This is illustrated by both age at retirement and years of retirement. The manufacturing retirees were offered a retirement package that accounts for the large percent retired in the four-to-five year cohort (over 29%).

Academic and professional retirees included 21% spouses and an overall mix that was nearly 50%/50% male and female. Manufacturing responders were entirely retirees, 94% male and only 6% female.

Over half of the manufacturing retirees reported annual household incomes (before taxes and from all sources) in the range from $15,000 to $45,000. The income distribution for academic and professional retirees is broader, with just over half of the retirees reporting annual household incomes in the range from $15,000 to $60,000.

Blue-collar personnel made up over 50% of the manufacturing responders. The two largest populations of academic and professional retirees were administrative/professional and faculty for a total of approximately 67%.

Table B-1 Comparative Demographics

	Manufacturing	Academic and Professional
Average Age:	Age (years)	Age (years)
Current age	62.1	73.0
Age at retirement	56.4	63.7
Years of retirement	5.7	9.3
Gender:	Percent	Percent
A = Male	93.6	50.6
B = Female	6.4	49.4
	100	100
Current marital status:		
A = Married	91.5	70.6
B = Divorced	4.3	4.8
C = Widowed	4.3	19.9
D = Never Married	0.0	4.8
	100	100
Years of retirement:		
A = 0 to 1 year	8.0	7.1
B = 1 to 2 years	9.6	6.6
C = 2 to 3 years	1.6	7.1
D = 3 to 4 years	1.6	5.0
E = 4 to 5 years	29.4	6.6
F = 5 to 7 years	14.4	11.4
G = 7 to 10 years	13.9	15.1

H = 10 to 15 years	15.5	22.2
I = Over 15 years	<u>5.8</u>	<u>18.8</u>
	100	100

Annual household income (before taxes and from all sources):

A = 0 to $15,000	3.8	7.6
B = $15,000 to $30,000	27.3	16.4
C = $30,000 to $45,000	25.1	17.0
D = $45,000 to $60,000	19.7	17.4
E = $60,000 to $75,000	9.3	11.4
F = $75,000 to $90,000	7.1	10.0
G = $90,000 to $105,000	1.6	9.6
H = $105,000 to $120,000	2.7	4.4
I = $120,000 to $135,000	1.6	2.4
J = Over $135,000	<u>1.6</u>	<u>3.6</u>
	100	100

Retirement status:

Retiree	100	78.7
Spouse of a retiree	0.0	15.5
Spouse of a deceased retiree	0.0	<u>5.8</u>
	100	100

Spousal status:

Retired	100	86.2
Partially retired/employed	0.0	7.3
Employed	<u>0.0</u>	<u>6.4</u>
	100	100

Academic and Professional Position at Retirement:

A = Clerical	15.4
B = Service	12.8
C = Administrative/Professional	28.7
D = Faculty	38.2
E = Other	<u>4.8</u>
	100

Manufacturing Position at Retirement:

A = Director or above	3.2
B = Manager	2.1
C = Department Head	3.2
D = Professional	5.9
E = Supervisor	23.0
F = Non-supervisory	36.4
G = Crafts/Trades	11.2
H = Assistant/Clerical	7.0
I = Support Service	4.8
J = Other	<u>3.2</u>
	100

Domains

The most important information about retirees came from their responses to short statements about ordinary life situations. Responses ranged from "strongly disagree" to "strongly agree" in five increments. The responses were analyzed with standard statistical techniques in SPSS, a computer program for statistics and data management. Exploratory Factor Analysis (EFA) was used to reduce the large number of interrelated variables to a small number of factors, herein referred to as domains. The items that make up any given domain are highly correlated.

Quartimax Rotation was used to identify the factors. Only those with eigenvalues of 1.5 or higher were selected; factor loadings of 0.5 or higher were used to identify 37 items within the factors. No items were repeated across factors.

The domains that define the manufacturing retirement environment are identical to those that define the academic and professional retirement environment. These domains are given below in relative order of importance:

Rank	Domain
1.	Freedom and Leisure (F & L)
2.	Finances (F)
3.	Work (W)
4.	Family and Friends (F & F)
5.	Health (H)
6.	Helping Others (HO)

Domain Scores

Once the domains were identified, mean values for each domain score were calculated. These scores provide normative information and allow for various tests, such as significance between populations, gender, time duration, etc.

The domain scores are given in Table B-2 for the combined retiree population as well as the separate cohorts. Standard deviations are included for reference.

Table B-2 Domain Scores

Domain	Combined (N=698)		Manufacturing (N=189)		Academic and Professional (N=509)	
	Mean	SD+	Mean	SD	Mean	SD
Freedom & Leisure	3.95	0.61	4.01	0.52	3.93	0.65
Finances	3.41	0.88	3.13*	0.85	3.52*	0.87
Work	3.15	0.50	3.15	0.50	3.15	0.51
Family & Friends	3.70	0.63	3.60**	0.68	3.74**	0.61
Health	3.27	0.47	3.27	0.47	3.28	0.47
Helping Others	2.95	0.87	2.82**	0.79	3.00**	0.89

+ Standard Deviation (SD) is a statistical measure of dispersion, or error, in the mean values.

* t-test shows significant difference at 0.001 level

** t-test shows significant difference at 0.01 level

Within the domain scores five items were reverse coded. For these, most retirees disagreed with the content of the statement as worded. The numeric scale for these five items was reversed in the final survey. Thus, if two retirees' scores in the same domain are compared, the higher score is an indication of a more positive response (higher agreement with the content of the domain).

Table B-2 indicates that the domain scores for manufacturing and academic and professional retirees are virtually the same in the domains of freedom and leisure, work and health. There are significant differences in their attitudes toward their retirement income, staying close to family and friends, and volunteerism in the community. Of these, feelings about retirement income reflect the annual incomes reported in Table B-1.

All domains correlate positively with happiness in retirement. A more positive domain score indicates a higher degree of happiness.

All domain scores are constant for approximately 10 years, then begin to drop off. The first decade of retirement corresponds with the happiest time for most retirees.

Domains also were tested for gender differences. Only the Helping Others domain shows a weak difference between male and female retirees. For example, among manufacturing retirees the mean domain scores for helping others were 2.79 (male) and 3.27 (female), significant at the 0.05 level. This same pattern was repeated within the academic and professional retirees.

Finally, one might ask why certain items from the survey were not included in any of the domains. The following examples belong to specific domains but did not correlate highly enough to be included:

> Freedom and Leisure
>> I can't wait to see what the next few years will bring.
>> Reading new books and magazines always interests me.
>> I have enjoyed a movie in the last few months.
>> I enjoy a glass of wine or beer.
>
> Finances
>> Compared to pre-retirement, my expenses are about the same.
>> My health insurance is excellent.
>
> Work
>> I miss daily contact with members of my department
>
> Family and Friends
>> My parents are not a burden to me.
>> Religious activities are an important part of my life.
>
> Health
>> I enjoy good health.
>> I am optimistic about the future.
>
> Helping Others
>> I can't wait to see what the next few years will bring.
>> I contribute something to a major charity every year.

These items drew strong responses—positive and negative—from many retirees but not enough to be included in the domains that define the retirement environment.

Transitions during Retirement

All domains are stable over the first decade of retirement. In every case, the domain score is constant for approximately 10 years, then begins to weaken.

Individual life situations that make up the domains are less stable over time. While many of them exhibit good stability over the first decade of retirement, others show definite trends. Qualitative analysis of these trends is given in Table B-3.

For example, retirement income looks great for the first two or three years; then the perception changes. The first few years of retirement are the "busiest"; there is no room for boredom. This peaks around the third year. At this same time comes a peak commitment to stay in your own community.

Many retirees report a weight gain around the second or third year into retirement. A correction quickly follows in years three to four to "balance diet and exercise to keep my weight under control."

Volunteerism also peaks around year three. This is counterbalanced by a steady shift in attitude throughout retirement: "I have taken on too many volunteer activities."

Table B-3 What Happens Next?

A. Early Transitions (peak around two to four years into retirement)

> My retirement income is greater than my current expenses.
>
> I am often bored with retirement.
>
> I plan to reside permanently in my current community.
>
> I am considering relocation to a different community.
>
> My weight has increased in recent years.
>
> Volunteering a few hours every week is important to me.

B. Steady Declines throughout Retirement

> I am optimistic about the future.
>
> I should have retired sooner than I did.
>
> My spouse/significant other thinks I should have retired sooner than I did.

C. Steady Increase throughout Retirement

> I have taken on too many volunteer activities.

D. Precipitous Drops (around 10 years into retirement)

> I like to learn something new every day.

> I have sufficient drive and energy to start new projects.

> During the last year, I enjoyed a vacation away from home.

> I am rarely bored with retirement.

Retirees report that their optimism and vigor decline continuously throughout retirement. They also conclude gradually that their prior goal of early retirement becomes less and less important.

Precipitous declines occur in several life situations around the 10th year of retirement. Vacation travel, drive and energy, and the need to keep learning drop off sharply; for some, boredom and depression set in.

Finally, a few things do not appear to change much across the retirement years. Patterns of exercise, health concerns, religious activities, and desire to be close to family and friends are bedrock values and activities that remain constant over the decades.

Appendix C
Reliability and Validity

Reliability. The most commonly used model of internal consistency is Alpha (Cronbach's Alpha), based on the average inter-item correlation. Experimental values of Cronbach's Alpha given below are considered to be a highly satisfactory measure of reliability:

Population	Alpha
Combined	0.846
Manufacturing	0.816
Academic and Professional	0.856

Validity. Validity is a subjective concept: Does the survey instrument measure what it is intended to measure? Two principal measures of validity were explored by comparing the content of independent narratives written by the retirees to "tell their story" with specific survey results.

Face Validity. Are the survey topics the "right topics" for retirees? Original field research and a preliminary survey (N=35) were used to identify preliminary scales with five to eight items in each. Individual scales and items were revised extensively before the final survey was sent out. Content of the narratives focused on identical concepts and content that were used to create the survey; the only exception was an occasional comment about married life.

Construct Validity. Two independent reviewers read 527 narratives. The frequency of topics that were written by retirees in free form was recorded and averaged. These results are given in Table C-1.

Table C-1 Frequency Analysis of Narrative Themes

Domain	Combined (N=1030) %	Manufacturing (N=365) %	Academic/ Professional (N=665) %
Freedom & Leisure	36.3	33.2	38.0
Finances	20.9	26.3	17.9
Health	13.1	12.1	13.7
Family & Friends	10.3	11.0	9.9
Work	10.1	12.6	8.7
Helping Others	9.3	4.9	11.7
	100	100	100

The principal comparison is the frequency of narrative comments to the content of the domains. Only six themes were found in the narratives, and they correspond exactly to the domains. The content of Domain 1, Freedom and Leisure, was cited most frequently in the narratives. Financial matters were cited next frequently. The order of the other domains varies somewhat from those identified in the survey, but the narrative content is identical to the domain content.

The conclusion is that the Grace Retirement Inventory (GRI) is a valid measure of the retirement environment.